"Without Mr. Pfaff, I would not be pursuing my dreams at USC. He is the type of teacher that does not only teach you in the classroom setting, but he challenges and motivates you to be a better version of yourself. He made it possible for me to be the first person in my family to go to college and I know that he will open up that path for many students to come. He is invested in his students and has a passion for teaching: a quality that not many teachers have." - Ariel Vieira, former student, pre medical student – USC

"Fantastic school guidance, but what's equally impressive is Mike's ability to help one navigate through the maze that is life." - Lat Le, former student, pre-medical/psychology student – UMASS

"Mr. Pfaff was one of my favorite teachers in high school because he always managed to make learning both fun and meaningful. In The Student Within, Mr. Pfaff presents some great strategies to help all students find enjoyment and meaning in their educational pursuits!" - Elle Fanning, former student, actress

"Everyone needs a purpose in life and "The Student Within" can help guide one through the path of self-realization, motivation, and reflection. So inspirational and thought-provoking! Mr. Pfaff's real-life experiences as well as his passion, perseverance, and generosity will empower young adults in finding their own life purpose and inner strength to become a better version of themselves. And if you ever feeling lost, read Mr. Pfaff's takeaways!" - Thao Nguyen, former student, Registered Nurse

"Mike Pfaff perfectly captures the inner struggle a student feels, and offers detailed and valuable advice on how to develop a personalized plan to navigate this crucial point in a person's life. The wisdom in this book is exactly the type of advice I would have wanted to hear in high school, but it is now perfectly laid out in a comprehensive and accessible way. Being a former student of Mr. Pfaff, I can say that I am proud he has created an effective medium to share his knowledge on education; I hope anyone who reads this book takes the lessons to heart. As a premedical student at Stanford University, who is dealing with his own struggles and hardships, I can truly say that education is personalized and *The Student Within* offers a flexible set of guidelines. Good luck on your journey ahead." - Eric Smith, former student, pre medical student – Stanford

"Mr. Pfaff was one of the main highlights my junior year of high school. He made me excited to come to class and learn! He was so encouraging not only in the classroom, but also outside of the classroom. Mr. Pfaff doesn't only care for his students' academic achievements, but for each individual's personal growth achievements. I can honestly say that he set a standard for what I look for in engaging professors as I wrap up my senior year of college, even as I look to get my Masters next fall." -   Esther Mugwanya, former student, social work - University of Texas

THE STUDENT WITHIN

WITHIN

The Art and Science of Easier Learning

Mike Pfaff

Edited and Designed by Judy Corcoran
www.judycorcoran.com
judycorc@gmail.com

Long Run Books &
Scribes Unlimited, LLC
2652 Ashurst Rd
Cleveland OH 44118
www.scribesunlimited.com
info@scribesunlimited.com

Printed in January 2019

For my mother.

Thank you for showing me that the best kind of teaching always comes straight from the heart. Your fierce dedication, courageous intellect, and empathetic nature has made a positive impact on thousands of student lives. We love you.

ACKNOWLEDGEMENTS

To Harry R. Groves and the Penn State Track team.
Thank you for instilling in me the work ethic,
camaraderie, and courage it takes to succeed at anything
you put your mind to.

To Matt Malone. You exemplify grit. You once said that
as a teacher, you don't always get to see the caterpillar
turn into a butterfly, but you always have to know that it
does. You were right.

To Julian Bull. Here's to living life with purpose.
Thank you for your inspiring leadership.

To Lisa Genova. A piece of inspiration in life is
priceless. You inspired me to do something I never
thought I could do. Thank you.

To Mark Salata. Thank you for your thoughtful advice,
encouragement and unwavering friendship. You've
always put the focus where it belongs in education, on
what's best for kids.

To my dad. Your sense of honor and steadfast loyalty to
those you love are immeasurable, not to mention your
sense of humor is priceless. Since I'm writing two more
books, "the best is always yet to come."

To my wife. Thank you for all your love, unwavering support, and contagious creativity. You've always challenged me to be the best version of myself. I love you.

To my beautiful daughter. Words can't articulate how much I love you. Even at two years old, you exemplify genuine empathy, loving gratitude, and unbounded joy. I'm so proud to be your father.

To my students. You inspire me to do more, give more, and be more. Without all of you, I would not have strengthened my own intrapersonal intelligence, thus bringing me closer to a joyous life filled with purpose.

Table of Contents

INTRODUCTION

I was never a great student in high school. It had nothing to do with the beautifully diverse, public, urban school I attended in Hackensack, New Jersey, in the 1990s. It had more to with me. Actually, it had all to do with me. I wasn't a bad student, I just wasn't that good. My overall high school GPA was around a low B.

In school, I usually opted for a quick, half-hearted attempt at homework in the morning during homeroom or during lunch on the day it was due. Classes that I could breeze through, such as driver's ed, auto shop, and lifeguard training (which also happened to give me a gym credit) made more sense to me. Most of the other classes felt like a chore.

My real passion was always athletics and by the time I got into high school, I focused in on cross country and track. I had some talent as a distance runner, but that wasn't what helped me excel to an elite level. It was the toughness I developed through the daily act of running, which not only included hard workouts and races against other talented athletes, but the energy I soaked in by seeing others exemplify acts of courage, grit and passion in sport.

Through athletics, I learned early on that inspiration could be contagious. I just didn't know that same energy and grit could be applied to other areas in my life until I accepted a NCAA Division 1 athletic scholarship to run for Penn State University. Once there, I began to see the connection. Through daily academic challenges, a lot of trial and error, and observing others exemplify determination and resiliency to achieve intellectual success, I began to understand that the life-force behind education was the same as with athletics.

Grit can be learned, taught, cultivated, motivated and applied anywhere and with anything you want to achieve. It's those principles that empowered me to serve as captain of Penn State's cross country and track teams before heading to Boston to embark on further education, not just in grad school, but in life.

In life, you will inevitably experience failures, disappointments and tragedies. If you don't, then you're not really living. The real education that results from grit will empower you not only to overcome those challenges, but to see them as gifts that you use to your full advantage. After all, it was a personal tragedy in my life that liberated me to clearly see my purpose and write this book.

If you asked the guys I grew up with if they ever thought I'd be teaching high school science, let alone writing a book, they'd probably laugh. I can't blame them. How were they supposed to know me back then when I didn't even know myself?

FOREWORD

"Never let your schooling get in the way of your education."

— Mark Twain

What do you want out of school right now?

Do you want to get straight A's in high school and beyond or do you just want to be a better student in general? Perhaps you want to get more enjoyment out of your learning experiences in high school or maybe you just want to figure out how you can create more free time. Whatever your reasons, the answer is — you can have it all.

Applying, not just knowing, the strategies in this book will not only empower you to make better use of time by prioritizing, organizing and taking action-driven steps, but it will put you on the path toward the most powerful education tool available — yourself. The best part of all is you do not have to work "harder," you just have to work "smarter."

Smart Defined

What does it mean to be or work smart? Is a smart person the one who gets straight A's in school? Perhaps a smart person is someone who can just pick up an article or textbook, read it once, and recall all the information in it. Maybe a smart person is the one who designs their own app in middle school and begins making $1,000 a week in

9

passive income selling it on iTunes? Or possibly a smart friend (we all seem to have one of these) seems to be able to talk their way out of any difficult situation, especially when they're in trouble. (By the way, this is a GREAT friend to have if you ever find yourself in a tangle.) Is smart the person who grew up in a bilingual home, took a third language in high school, and now fluently speaks three languages? Or is it a person who can perform a long, complex sequence of dance moves after seeing and trying the dance routine just a few times. Maybe smart is that friend who taught themselves how to play the guitar by fidgeting around with a hand-me-down axe in their free time. The answer is – they are ALL smart. And WE are all smart.

The problem I've seen with most students is they limit their definition of smart due to the emphasis that school systems put on "logical-mathematical" intelligence, a term pioneered by Howard Gardner, who proposed the theory of multiple intelligences. Logical-mathematical intelligence focuses on a student's ability to recall abstract visual information and use numbers to reason, analyze and solve problems. As a result, students begin to attach more value to this one type of intelligence while devaluing the others. Or worse, they fail to even recognize that a whole plethora of other intelligences exist.

Without the self-recognition and acknow-ledgment that each person has different innate faculties (strengths) that exist at various levels, then you can struggle to tap into, apply, cultivate and motivate your own talents and skills. If that one type of logical-mathematical intelligence isn't one of your more dominant strengths, then you can begin to struggle with teaching and assessment tools that emphasize that type of strength. Consequently, you can develop a lower sense of self in the classroom, and sometimes in life.

The equivalent to this scenario would be taking Michael Jordan, arguably the best basketball player ever, and putting him on the baseball field in the prime of his career and saying he's an average athlete. Or worse, taking Michael Jordan and putting him into a water polo competition or ballet performance and saying he sucks. Does Michael Jordan suck as an athlete? Of course not! He's Michael freakin Jordan! The problem is not only the assessment tool we used to "judge" Michael Jordan's athletic prowess, but it's that Jordan didn't take the time to cultivate his innate strengths to find the encouragement to master those other sports. I'm sure Jordan could have reached impressive levels of success in those other areas if he had been as passionate and devoted to them as he was to basketball.

Drawing From Within

The term "education" comes from the Latin root "educo," meaning "to draw from within." When we tap into our own natural talents and develop the associated skills, education or educo happens all the time over the course of our lives, not just in the classroom. When we learn to bridge this gap between drawing upon and leveraging our personal intelligence with what we're currently learning, then an amazing level of academic and personal success can be achieved in the classroom and in life. I have personally seen countless examples of how self-analysis has brought a student's success level both in and out of the classroom to enormous slam-dunk heights.

So how can you be Michael Jordans of the classroom? How can you make the game of school your main sport, the game you were meant to play? The answer lies in Aristotle's famous words, "know thyself."

How We Think

Ponder these three words for a moment – think about thinking. Think about how your own brain works. What kinds of activities seem to come naturally to you? What kinds of compliments do you get from friends, family, even strangers that you just brush off because whatever you were complimented on seemed so effortless and easy to you that you didn't think twice about it, let alone accept a compliment on it. Now think about what those activities or compliments might be. It can be something as seemingly insignificant as, "how do you remember the words to that song?" "Can you tell me if these clothes match?" Maybe you're the person friends always go to for advice, especially when it comes to relationships. Or perhaps you're that Grand Theft Auto player with a 215 ranking that keeps sniping me from a rooftop because you've cracked every code there is to be cracked. The examples are endless. The more important point is they are all examples of "intelligence."

In the next few chapters, I'll walk you through the different types of intelligence and give you examples of how others have used their own innate skills and talents to work smarter and learn more easily. There is an art and science to learning, and since I work in both science, as a teacher, and the arts, as an actor, I have a unique perspective on this. My hope is that you not only discover your own unique intelligence, but that you uncover the inevitable passion to unleash specific talents that take you to your highest levels of smart.

CHAPTER 1 Your Teachers Are Good People

"You can't win a kid's mind until you win their heart."

> *- Matt Malone, superintendent of*
> *Fall River Public Schools and*
> *former Massachusetts Secretary of*
> *Education*

Statistically speaking, teachers (especially professors) in our country are some of the most overeducated and underpaid professionals out there. According to the latest data from the Bureau of Labor Statistics, the median annual wage for high school teachers, of which most have advanced degrees in education, was $58,030. Clearly, something else draws them to the field of education.

Ninety-nine percent of the time, teachers are drawn to the field for the right reasons – to help students. Why else would teachers spend so much time preparing for class outside of work, bring mounds of paperwork home, grade endless papers, projects, labs and tests, and eat packed lunches while they work? Teachers get up early, dress professionally, work tirelessly and always seem to have a smile on their faces (hopefully). Plus, my mom is a teacher and Oprah Winfrey loves teachers, so you know they've got to be great! However, the learning process can often be a painful compromise between a student and teacher.

Teachers have authority in their classroom and are constantly demanding more of their students to think, act and work longer, harder and more effectively. At times, the result can be a negative perception of what a teacher represents because you are being pushed out of your comfort zone. If this has happened to you with any specific teacher (I'm sure you have one in mind), I urge you to take a step back and ask yourself why. Why might your teacher demand your attention, enforce behavioral norms in the classroom, nag you to get in assignments, subtract points for errors, not accept late work, and assert punishments for infractions? Believe it or not, it's because they care about you.

The most important part of a teacher's job is to prepare you for the rigors of what awaits you when you graduate, whether it's college, trade school, the military, a job, traveling, parenting, volunteer work or anything in between. It's important you remember that fact because it will inform how you approach your work with them and could even inform how you approach your work after them. How you see your teachers matters. If you see where they are truly coming from, you won't see the trials they place on you as negative and you will be more open to challenge and growth.

The first year I taught at South Boston High School (renamed the South Boston Educational Complex and broken into three smaller schools), an extremely disheartening event happened outside the building. A nameless, faceless coward spray painted racist graffiti on the high school outside walls. It was heart breaking to everyone – the faculty, people in the community, but especially the students. Racist propaganda anywhere would have a profoundly negative effect on any community and the country as a whole. And with South Boston, we're talking about a school that didn't go through desegregation until 1975! Riots about busing people of color to the school used to break out in front of the building on a daily basis.

Believe it or not, my mentor teacher, who only retired a few years ago, starting teaching there when African Americans weren't allowed in the school due to the color of their skin. It's hard to believe such extreme bigotry was not only part of our country's school norm, but it happened so recently. At the same time, maybe it's not hard to believe, given the kind of prejudicial behavior that still exists in our society today. Regardless, that specific act of hatred at South Boston high school, especially given the history there, needed to be dealt with immediately.

Our school principal at the time, Dr. Matt Malone, called every social service agency in the city and held a big assembly for all students, faculty and social service agencies in the Boston area. Different speakers came during that assembly to express their voice of love, tolerance and community. Then Dr. Malone, a former US marine, spoke to the whole school about how to recognize prejudice in subtle forms in addition to the blatant ones. He then expressed a message to every student straight from his heart, "I will risk my life to make sure every student who comes into this school is safe." Those of us who knew him knew he wasn't kidding.

It's my belief that a guardian and youth advocate like Dr. Malone exists in every educator. It is what draws the people of goodness into this field.

Teaching, itself, is such an extension of one's own good personality. That is not something to be taken lightly.

Teachers And School Systems

It's important to recognize the distinction between school systems and how they traditionally operated and the human beings that are your teachers who work in them. Believe it or not, school systems were traditionally built on a factory model which resembled prisons, a system based on fear to create a tolerant, civilized society.

Think about it, most schools have a firm bell schedule, grade levels based on age, classes with a specific scope and sequence for everyone, credit requirements to advance, etc. In addition, school systems have punitive measures for infractions which can go as far as suspension and expulsion, the ultimate rejection.

Even though research supports that positive reinforcement is much more effective than punishment, school systems, not necessarily teachers, seem to put more of an emphasis on punishing for infractions than rewarding for accomplishments. As a result, it's possible to blur the distinction between your teachers and the school. If you go into every class and mentoring situation understanding that distinction, then you'll remember during times of struggle that your teachers and mentors are human beings coming from a good place and you'll resist the urge to make a negative generalization and self-create an adversarial relationship.

Even if you have legitimate cases of a teacher behaving unfairly, you will still have a better outcome if you see all teachers as facilitators who are helping to guide you to the best version of yourself. Ultimately, you are responsible to draw from within – your "educo" – and your teachers are facilitators who challenge you to think, create, and learn along your own journey.

Personally, my first-year teaching at South Boston High school was my wake-up call into what it truly means to be a teacher. I had previously worked for a software company just months before my first full year in the classroom. I had obtained my Master's degree in education part time at night while I was working full time for a software company and then was fortunate enough to win a scholarship program for the Massachusetts Institute for New Teachers (MINT), a program designed to pull passionate professionals from other occupations and place them in high-need public school districts. I completed my teaching practicum over a six-week period in the summer at Charlestown High School for students retaking algebra and then shortly after that, I was thrown into the fire. It's where my heart and mind wanted to be.

My first full year I was tasked with teaching "active" physics (mainly conceptual based) to a large, diverse group of inner-city freshmen. I quickly learned that no number of graduate courses and theories on best teaching practices would prepare me for what awaited. But I did connect with the students right away. After all, I was in their same exact seat when I was a freshman at an urban, diverse public high school in Hackensack, New Jersey, just 10 years earlier.

While I was bursting with energy and enthusiasm and over-planned every lesson, I still had difficulty getting everyone's full attention. Classroom management was an issue, a big issue. It was disappointing to work so hard to prepare engaging lessons to teach and inspire kids only to spend half the class time handling behavioral issues. It was at that time of struggle that I remembered what my principal told me the first day I started. "You can't win a kid's mind until you win their heart." So, I took that statement to heart (pun intended) and decided to take a slightly unorthodox approach.

Dr. Zandango

I created an alter ego, a character, who was a zany, comedic, old, raspy voiced scientist by the name of Dr. Zandango. I bought an old white wig and beard, wore big rimmed glasses, ordered a lab coat with a big "Z" on the back and even had professional embroidery on the front of the coat which said "official performer of the Zandango Fandango." Was I losing my mind?

Perhaps.

The first day of class that I decided to bring in my alter ego, the class had no warning. I simply told them that I invited a professor to the school from "Science University" to explain a new concept we'll be getting into – Newton's Laws of motion. Another teacher friend stepped into my class for a few minutes while I stepped out to change into character. As I walked down the hallway toward my class dressed as Dr. Zandango, I did receive some strange looks from other faculty, especially the veteran teachers. However, I stayed the course because my goal was simple – win their hearts. Needless to say, when I re-entered the classroom, I had the student's full attention. In fact, one could literally hear a pin drop in that class of 31 tough, rowdy inner-city youth.

Dr. Zandango introduced himself and then began teaching the lesson for the day. As Dr. Zandango proceeded, I quickly realized something miraculous happening in the class. The students got extremely engaged and went along for the ride. Even though most of the students quickly caught on that this crazy character was me (yes, believe it or not, a few of my students couldn't tell), they still played along, almost like I was Santa Clause spreading some holiday cheer. Each student respectfully raised their hands to answer questions, politely asked their own questions, and really wanted to prove to Dr. Zandango that they understood the concepts he was teaching.

If the majority of students demonstrated comprehension by the end of the lesson, then Dr. Zandango would do a little dance called the "Zandango-Fandango," which was basically a mix between the Pee Wee Herman "Tequila" dance and my own compilation of '90s break dancing moves I picked up over the years. In addition, Dr. Zandango had a clear policy on behavior. If the class misbehaved, he would leave and get Mr. Pfaff who would come back into the class and clear house. Needless to say, it worked like a charm.

I started bringing out my Dr. Zandango character about once a week and every single time I did my classroom transformed from a rowdy, high school class into a graduate level college lecture hall. Dr. Zandango became so popular that he even partnered with Boston University to bring tons of interactive physics demonstrations and lead a school wide assembly for nearly a thousand students to prepare them for the school's annual Science Fair.

At one point, I even considered demanding separate paychecks for Dr. Zandango from Human Resources, but I figured that might be going too far (just kidding…maybe). So, what's the point of revealing this borderline-certifiable insane teaching tactic that I clearly did not learn in graduate school? The point is, I was able to win my student's hearts.

My students saw that because I was willing to make a fool of myself to reach and teach them, they would decide to give me their minds to the best of their ability. Even when Dr. Zandango wasn't in the class, my students would reference him occasionally and were way more invested and focused while making a much stronger overall effort. Work quality, both inside and outside of the class, went up dramatically that year. It's been years since I've turned into my alter ego, but I still have my whole Dr. Zandango outfit in a plastic bag in my closet because, well, you never know.

In addition, to this day I have former students, who are now turning 30, who still mention Dr. Zandango to me over FB and thank me with a laugh. What's the takeaway from this story? It's that **your heart is connected to your mind**. It will ultimately lead you to discover your passion. And if you can find a way to open your heart to your teacher, you'll be amazed how it not only positively changes your perception of them, but engages your mind to its fullest capacity.

Perceptions

If you're still skeptical about the possible bias you might be carrying that can lead to incorrect judgments, misunderstandings and costly mistakes involving teachers, then let's take a look at the science behind it. A fascinating article was published in *Nature Neuro Science* (May, 2016) by Jonathan Freeman. The results of the study conducted at New York University revealed how we perceive and remember a person's face is greatly influenced by the stereotypes we have of them. Researchers monitored brain activity through an MRI to see how participants would remember a person's feelings, based on their expression, after seeing it for just a short glimpse.

Participants were asked to perceive and recall those emotions of various people who differed in race and gender. Even though all participants took a conscious survey before this controlled experiment to prove they didn't carry any bias, do you know what the actual results of the test revealed? Bias, extreme bias. For example, most participants in the study remembered men, particularly black men, as being angry even though the faces of the black men shown to them were all neutral. In addition, most of the participants perceived and remembered the expressions of the pictures of women they saw as being happy, even though those pictures of expression were neutral as well.

We have undisputable scientific evidence that supports the fact that the tendency of humans is to perceive other people as having bias, but consistently fail to recognize the bias within ourselves. Why is that? It's because our opinion of ourselves are based on our own self-awareness (or lack thereof it), thoughts and assumed beliefs. We tend to judge others by their actions and judge ourselves by our intentions. The result is a failure to recognize our own prejudices that could negatively affect how we perceive reality.

That fact reminds me of what the famous Hollywood acting teacher, Howard Fine, teaches his students when they're trying to find the humanity in any character they are playing. "Do not judge the character, justify him," Howard would say. Even if the character you're portraying is a serial killer, justify his actions by looking for his reasons rather than judging him for what he does.

What's the result of that important self-reflective character analysis an actor must do for a truthful performance? The portrayal of a character we can all relate to who can evoke empathy from an audience, even if he is a serial killer, because he has been humanized.

We are all human and we can improve our perceptions of reality by taking a close look at our own bias. So, ask yourself an honest question – do you carry any negative stereotypes about teachers? Perhaps you unconsciously assume they might lack compassion, a sense of humor, are too strict, or are just a plain 'ole nerd. How might that have an impact on instructions, redirection or questions they might ask? I've personally seen countless examples of students in the same class, interpreting the same event very differently, based on their own preconceived ideas.

Whatever preconceived notions you might be carrying, if you can recognize and reconcile any bias you might have about your teachers, your present experiences with them will consistently seem more positive, supportive and even inspiring.

Lastly, while we can often have discrepancy in the quality of schooling a student may receive between demographics, districts, types of schools, etc., we all still get that opportunity in the United States. Compare that to the approximately 70 million children around the world who have no opportunity to even go to school, especially those living in North Eastern Africa. In Somalia, only 10% of the children go to some kind of primary school. Also, in those poor countries, girls are far less likely to attend school then boys.

Sometimes we don't truly appreciate what we have until we've traveled to a third world country with an outreach program or simply volunteered at a soup kitchen in our home town to feed the homeless. Philanthropy will improve your intelligence and perspective because failure to recognize the advantages you have in this country is unintelligent, whether you're attending a public school in urban America, a charter school in the Midwest, or a private school on the west coast.

Remember, teachers are good people. They choose the profession for a number of reasons, one of the most obvious reasons is they want to make a difference in young people's lives. They have a deep desire to help people. Even if they appear to be intimidating, tough and uncompromising, you need to ask yourself "where is that coming from?" If you search deeply enough, you'll see it's coming from a place of love and a desire from the heart to help people.

While a teacher's way of helping might not always appeal to your desires, they are still there to help. Your ability to recognize this is imperative for your growth not only as a student, but as a human being. Einstein once said, "The most important decision we make is whether we believe we live in a friendly or hostile universe." Do you see the universe and the people in it as friendly? If your answer to this question is yes, then inevitably you will have an easier time, not only in the classroom, but life. Knowing this fact will empower you to get through those class times that at first glance, might seem too difficult, unfair or stressful.

Remember your education isn't always going to be easy. As you get to know yourself better in this process, it might seem effortless and fun at times. At other times, it might seem complex, confusing and overwhelming. It's these times that you have to remember the fundamental truths about your education and all the facilitators, your teachers being one of them, around you whom are helping you to gain further insight.

MR. PFAFF'S TAKEAWAYS

- Recognizing the goodness in your teachers will make you more receptive to learning.

- Your heart is connected to your mind.

- Make the distinction between your teachers and the physical school where they work.

- Teachers and schools aren't automatically provided to all kids in the world.

CHAPTER 2 The Value of Mindset

"If you love life, don't waste time, for time is what life is made up of."

Bruce Lee, actor, martial artist, activist

What is mindset? According to Carol Dweck, a professor of psychology at Stanford University, mindset as it relates to our educational growth can be placed into two different categories, "growth" or "fixed." Ask yourself – if you were going to invest some money with the hopes of making more in the future, would you want it to be based on fixed (in other words, limited) potential or growth potential? Chances are, you opted for growth potential.

Dweck sees mindset in the same way. She believes that one who has a "fixed mindset" sees abilities, either their own or someone else's, as something that they were born with and cannot acquire or develop during their lifetime. On the contrary, Dweck sees a "growth mindset" as one who sees abilities as something that can be acquired if enough time and effort are invested. While I do agree with this philosophy, my experiences working with thousands of teenage students has taught me that specific tools must be given to all students, especially those who may be operating, if even on a partial level, within a fixed mindset.

We are all students when it comes to learning to draw from within ourselves, and if you don't see how you can utilize your own innate strengths to acquire comprehension and knowledge, then you will never believe time and effort can produce a result. In fact, you won't even be motivated to try. As a result, a lot of your valuable lifetime can be wasted in an inefficient manner which doesn't serve your growth as a learner.

However, if as a student, you empower yourself to recognize and utilize your own innate strengths, then you will immediately start to see the sparks of a fire that inevitably lead to a roaring blaze. It's that fire, that motivation that will place your mindset in a growth category, allowing you to take full advantage of your lifetime and reach the potential you're destined for in every situation.

Getting On Track

It's important to recognize that the initial spark that sets you on the right path toward education is never a huge event. In fact, if you're not paying attention, you can often miss it. That transition into a growth mindset always starts with a small, private victory before it becomes more apparent to the outside world. Do you think tennis great Serena Williams fired serves at 128 miles per hour, executed backhand drives with impeccable form, and positioned herself perfectly on the court before she had a private victory in which she learned to master basic footwork and stroke mechanics?

Of course not.

As a student, small private victories are often as simple as recognizing in yourself that you retain and often enjoy studying more with a friend because you've discovered you're more of an interpersonal learner. More importantly, that small victory would involve action on your part, such as scheduling regular, on-going study sessions with one or more friends either in person or over the internet. Perhaps you realize that you tend to comprehend and recall information more easily when it's presented visually because you have a strong faculty as a visual-spatial learner.

Therefore, you begin sketching concepts on paper to connect ideas while using drawing techniques, playing imagination games and watching teaching videos. Maybe you've discovered that you do better when you're able to listen, read, write or talk about information in order to make better sense of the content you're studying because you're a strong verbal-linguistic learner. As such, you decide to start taping class lectures and listening to them again on your own time. In addition, audio books, regular discussions with peers and journal writing sessions becomes your norm to internalize content.

Tapping Into Yourself

The various examples are endless, but they all have one common theme: They begin with analysis and recognition of self to tap into your personal resources. When you tap into your personal resources, you can't help but to achieve success not only by learning more, but by enjoying the process itself.

It's very clear at this point for any learner to make the connection between the specific action you took to learn and the positive outcome you experienced as a result. Thus, you see the time and effort you invested as worthwhile and you do it again. A growth mindset is born.

Mindset also has a broader meaning besides just the two categories relating to effort and time investment. It can be considered to be your world view and philosophy on life in general. As such, that philosophy informs your actions on both a conscious and subconscious level. However, what if some of your actions aren't serving you well or making your life better? What if some of your actions are hindering you in some way, preventing you from receiving the success, enjoyment and happiness you deserve? Then you have to embark on the courageous pathway toward change. Otherwise, you'll just keep doing things the way you always did them, instead of adapting and changing your actions to better serve you.

Often, however, we need to understand where our previous actions were coming from in order to change our current actions. Courage, strength and humility are needed to look at ourselves closely if we want to have a different mindset which will cause us to establish routine actions different from our norm. Is it worth it? You're damn right it is! Any positive change we make in our actions on a regular basis will have a profound impact on the quality of our lives. We can all greatly benefit from it. The process, however, is not easy.

Struggling To Bloom

I'll provide many examples that I've personally had with students in the chapters to come, but first, let's discuss a term I'm sure you're all familiar with: late bloomer. I don't like this term because it implies a person has yet to grow, blossom or become. In nature, however, plants often grow the most when they are under stress, not when everything is perfect. Similarly, you are growing the most under times of stress, not when the A's on tests, quizzes and various assessments come easily. If you don't believe me, ask yourself if you can remember what you learned, not what you already knew, on a test that you got an easy A on. The truth is the student who is learning, and therefore growing the most is the student who is struggling, being challenged and finding themselves.

Essentially, the student who often seems to be struggling the most can often be the student who is growing and learning about themselves internally the most. Embracing that struggle as a productive, necessary path on your journey will help you adapt to the right mindset as well.

Personally, I struggled with this a great deal growing up and as a young adult. My answer to anything that required me to self-analyze and change my mindset was simply to get busier. Looking back, I now know it's not only because self-analysis is hard and uncomfortable, it can even be scary. Reflecting back on certain periods in my life, I'm amazed at how hard I worked at avoiding a process that could have made my life so much easier and rewarding. For a stretch of about 10 years, I overworked myself to a maximum instead of slowing down to really analyze where my actions were coming from. I inundated myself with numerous responsibilities to avoid thinking about it.

My self-inflicted responsibilities weren't necessarily bad, but they were unfocused and pulled me in numerous directions, leaving me exhausted.

In addition, I didn't participate in any of them with moderation. For example, I received my Master's degree at night while I was working full time for a software company. At that same time, I had a part-time job working for a professor at the University where I was getting my masters, which I'd work on during weekday evenings and weekends.

In addition, I was competing for an elite post-collegian running team, Reebok Boston, and would race most weekends and attend practice weekday nights. While the routine actions I participated in as an athlete helped me reach success, it also caused damage because I didn't know myself well enough to analyze which routine actions were serving me and which might be hurting me.

My Own Track

In 2000, I won the JP Morgan Chase corporate challenge in Boston, a highly competitive race with over 15,000 runners. About six months later, I suffered a career ending knee injury. I tore my meniscus in my right knee. I had actually already torn my meniscus in both knees, both of which required surgery before that. However, that time it also resulted in osteoarthritis and osteonecrosis, which was more serious. My knee injury got so bad because I couldn't break my routine of running and training every day, despite the knee pain I was experiencing. As a result, a third knee surgery was required and I was never able to run pain free again after that.

Other sport injuries include popped hips, stress fractures in my foot and femur, countless torn ankles, a sports hernia that required surgery, a broken thumb during boxing, which required two surgeries, and most recently, atrial fibrillation which some physiologists contribute to extreme cardiovascular exercise. All of these conditions are due to overuse.

After my injury, I immediately filled the time I spent running by taking acting classes in improvisation at night instead. For six of those years after my injury, I simultaneously held three jobs. One job was as a full time AP biology and chemistry teacher within the Boston Public School System. After I finished teaching at the high school for the day, I went to another job as an adjunct professor at Suffolk University. The third job was that of a bartender at Boston Symphony Hall during a few weekday and weekend nights.

As I got more engrossed in the world of acting, I started to go to every possible audition I could and began booking jobs. First, I was working on student films certain weekends, which led to short films, then local commercials, and then various plays in Boston, NYC and even Scotland.

I continued the same exercise regime, working out two to three hours a day, but I didn't run the way I used to due to the knee injury. My self-inflicted busy schedule didn't allow me any real time to self-analyze, so it prevented me from finding my core, innate strengths, motivations and true desires. A lot of my energy was spent on achieving without any thought on what I really wanted, so no matter what I achieved, it wasn't enough. Clearly, I've repeated actions in my life that didn't always serve me. I needed a change of philosophy or mindset to slow down and really self-analyze my true desires, strengths and areas that needed development.

When I finally got off the crazy rollercoaster schedule I maintained, I decided to quit every job I had and move to Los Angeles to pursue an acting career. As crazy as that might sound to some people, pursuing the craft of acting forced me to spend a tremendous amount of time self-analyzing to connect, relate and empathize with the characters I was playing. It turned out to be one of the most valuable forms of education I ever received. It reconnected me to my own center and my own passions. Ironically, in the process, it also reignited that spark in me to teach and help students. Only that deep level of self-analysis could have led me to the purpose, fulfillment and joy I get from the work I now do today, both as a teacher of Science and a creative. My only wish was I had started sooner.

Celebrate Differences

My strong advice to you is don't wait and minimize the amount of your valuable lifetime you spend on things that are not in your heart or don't improve the quality of your life. Find the courage to look at yourself early and often. Don't just discover your own uniqueness, celebrate it! Because the truth is – we're all different and we're all unique. Just as we all have our own unique set of fingerprints, we all have a unique brain with specific, innate strengths, motivations and desires. When you take the necessary steps to understand your own brain, it will unlock unlimited potential in any area you wish to grown in. That kind of discovery and its resulting growth will empower and connect you more with the people you love and care about. It will put you on a continuous path toward the best version of yourself.

The benefits of self-analysis are the keys to the kingdom, literally. Understanding yourself more in-depth not only leads to enormous academic success and healthier, happier relationships, but it leads to better physical, spiritual and emotional health.

So why wait? If you're like me and most other people, self-analysis can be uncomfortable. Anything new, anything that requires you to think in a way you haven't done before will feel uncomfortable. It can even be fearful. What if, for example, you take a close look at yourself and discover, on your own, that your brain works very differently than most of your peers? That might be something you don't want to find out because it would be evidence that you are different from others.

If that example troubles you, then you're forgetting that just as we all physically look different, our minds are all different. Such a heavy emphasis and desire is placed on people, especially teenagers, to fit in. Regardless of race, nationality, creed or socio-economic status, all teenagers feel universal peer pressure to conform. In fact, most therapists will agree that all people really want at their core is to be accepted.

Taking the courageous time to think about your own brain with its own personal strengths and desires will help you overcome that influence because you will accept yourself. As such, any pressure you feel to conform will disappear because you will know yourself well enough to be confident and comfortable just by being you.

MR. PFAFF'S TAKEAWAYS

- Adopt a growth mindset in which you know your time and effort are worthwhile

- Leverage your personal strengths by utilizing learning techniques that compliment them.

- Develop the courage to self-analyze regularly.

CHAPTER 3   Intrapersonal Fuels All Intelligences

"Everyone is a genius. But if you judge a fish on its ability to climb a tree, it will live its whole life believing that it is stupid."

– Albert Einstein, scientist

A heavy emphasis is often placed on semantics within school systems. "Buzz" words trend among faculty members across school systems in the same manner music does with teenagers. I often hear our 12th grade students jamming in the senior patio to old school Tribe Called Quest, Slick Rick, Led Zeppelin, ACDC and Johnny Cash. Those are songs that were popular when I was in high school and even some of them were hits when my parents were in high school.

Words that define teaching and learning trend in the same fashion. New words with the same meanings replace old ones and old ones often get recycled. I remember in elementary school when the term "active reading" was popular. Now words such as "metacognition," "differentiated instruction," "higher order thinking," "scaffolding," "pedagogy," "peer assessment," and "common core" are a few of the leading buzz words. You might be asking yourself, "why is it even important that I'm aware of any of these words? It is teacher terminology and I don't plan on teaching, ever!" While that might very well be true, spending some time understanding and connecting to the meaning behind these words can empower you to surpass plateaus and put you on a path of consistent self-discovery. All those buzz words are essentially describing various learning processes.

Exploring and investigating various processes will be your key to unlocking your own potential as a learner.

Therefore, pay attention just as much to the different methods you use to learn content as to the content itself. This will help guide you to find your own unique and specific "bag of learning tricks." Once you're on that path, not only will learning become easier, but aspirations and dreams will be more within reach.

No matter what your current situation is, you alone own the power of your mind and the direction in which you choose to lead it. So, try to categorize the understanding of these words, or better yet, the processes behind them in the category of "education," not "schooling." When the emphasis is placed on understanding the true meaning behind the word, then you simply choose which word, or learning process, makes the most sense to you. Ironically, that takes some self-knowledge.

Types Of Intelligences

Howard Gardner really awakened all learners when he said the question we should be asking ourselves is not, "How smart are we?" but "How are we smart?" Gardner presented a series of "intelligences," ranging from intrapersonal, interpersonal, kinesthetic, musical, spatial, linguistic, naturalistic, existential – all the way to the one that can often be a student's nemesis in the school system – logical-mathematical.

We all have a combination of these strengths that determine what we're inherently good at and what we're not. If you're curious and starting to think about how your own brain works (the buzz word currently attached to this kind of thinking is "metacognition"), try this free self-assessment tool which only takes five minutes:

https://www.literacynet.org/mi/assessment/findyour strengths.html

Now that you've taken the self-assessment tool and scored a 100% for "kinesthetic" or possibly "musical" intelligence, does that mean you're going to be the next Serena Williams or Mozart? Not exactly. We all know that Mozart didn't just become the musical genius he was because he had a high predisposition for hearing and creating pleasant sounds. How would you explain Helen Keller's extraordinary success as an author, political activist and lecturer when she didn't even have the innate ability to see or hear? What led to their success, and what could lead to your own success, both in and out of the classroom, is **having a better understanding of where your own natural**

**faculties (talents) lie and how to utilize those
strengths by incorporating specific tools to your
own advantage.**

When students start learning how to do this, an
interesting phenomenon happens which I've seen
over and over and over again. They actually start to
enjoy the learning process more. They start to have
fun.

A stronger understanding of some of the
different ways our brains process information and
how we are all uniquely different with innate
abilities is necessary before we take a closer look at
what Gardner calls Intrapersonal Intelligence. When
we discuss a term such as Intrapersonal Intelligence,
think about how closely related it is to the old Latin
root "educo," which dates back to the 1800s.
Perhaps even more relevant to your life, think of a
term your parents or grandparents might have used
before – "self-reliance." In the end, the meaning of
these words is essentially the same – *Find your
power by drawing from within.*

When you really think about it, you'll realize
you are already aware of this eternal truth. While
outside situations, people, places and events might
have inspired or shaped your thinking in some way,
it was how you perceived those things internally
that shaped who you are.

So, is it as easy as just asking ourselves to do
something or anything we want to accomplish?

Well, would it be fair to ask someone else to perform a task without giving or showing them the necessary tools to do it? For instance, would you ask someone to change your flat tire with a butter knife and shoe laces and expect a successful outcome? If your answer was no, then you have to be fair with yourself when placing the same kinds of demands.

Finding The Right Tools

That being said, finding the correct tool for yourself isn't as simple as using the correct inanimate object for a given situation, such as a cross bar and jack for a flat tire. If you're an action movie fan, then think of it like the actor who played the T-1000 terminator (the "bad robot") in *Terminator 2*, Robert Patrick. He was a dynamic, fluid machine whose metal parts could liquefy into anything that was needed in the moment, constantly finding a new way to achieve a desired outcome. Your dynamic tool, your adaptable machine, is your consistent ability to discover and rediscover yourself – your strengths, your weaknesses, your personal sources of motivation and to utilize and leverage them to your advantage.

Whether you're more of a linguistic, musical, kinesthetic, visual-spatial, interpersonal, naturalistic or logical-mathematical learner, it will take intrapersonal knowledge/educo/self-reliance to know it.

Let's go back to the flat tire example. How fun and engaging would it be for you to attempt to change that flat tire with the butter knife and shoe laces? Chances are you'd get pretty frustrated, bored and disengaged fairly quickly. However, if you had a cross bar and jack and easily popped off the hub cap and got that first lug nut loose, chances are you'd experience a tiny sense of satisfaction, enough to motivate you to get the next lug nut loose and then the next one. Once you get all the lug nuts off and take the old tire off the rim, there is no way you're not going to be motivated to put the spare tire on. Once you get the new tire on, you're probably moving even faster to tighten those lug nuts and finish the job.

Take this analogy a step further and say you even knew where you were going when you got that flat tire, such as spring break to the beach for a few days with your best friends. Chances are you'd be changing that tire with more energy, enthusiasm and joy than you ever had before.

This situation is an analogy to how your potential to learn operates. Identifying and using your own unique tool box will not only get the job done, but it will help you discover where you ultimately want to go. Just getting a sense of direction, let alone discovering exactly where you want to go, will be one of the most self-motivating processes you can experience.

**Connecting With Your Own Specific Abilities
Can Help You Find That Direction.**

Cultivating motivation, by the way, is also an ability. Therefore, once you do it, you'll want to do it again and again and again. Next, you'll probably want to go to new places. You might even decide to travel out of the state, out of the country, out of the continent, or even off of the planet.

If you can recognize that we are all life-long learners and that our education has more to do with learning about ourselves (educo) than the simple regurgitation of facts we learn in the classroom, then you can achieve levels of academic and personal success that reach far beyond your imagination.

It's funny what society deems as "smart." Not only am I a high school teacher who teaches science at a private high school in the Valley in California, but I'm also an actor. Having taught in the Boston Public School system at South Boston High school for six years previous to moving out west, I've closely watched the career of Bostonian actor Matt Damon. Hollywood has often called Matt Damon one of the "smartest" A-list actors around.

However, I'm not sure if Hollywood was prepared to say that when Matt Damon dropped out of Harvard University to head to Los Angeles. In fact, society is often prepared to brand any person who decides to drop out of college as "unintelligent." But Matt dropped out of Harvard because he had enough intrapersonal intelligence to know what he wanted to pursue. He didn't let his schooling get in the way of his education. Clearly Matt Damon's knowledge of self and his "education" triumphed over "schooling" in his life.

I'm not advocating for students to drop out of school, but I am advocating to allow a deep understanding and knowledge of self to guide you through your life, both in and out of the classroom – even if that self-knowledge guides you down a path that might seem atypical to many.

> *"The unexamined life is not worth living"* –
> **Socrates**

Intrapersonal Intelligence

As an educator in various roles such as adjunct professor in educational psychology, high school physiology, physics, biology, and chemistry teacher, tutor and father, I have seen many people overcome, grow and achieve levels of academic and life success that would astound you. The largest determinant of that success always falls under one major intelligence that is often overlooked within the traditional school system – intrapersonal intelligence.

As Gardner describes it, **intrapersonal intelligence** (not to be confused with interpersonal intelligence) **is found in "people who are aware of**

their emotions, motivations, beliefs and goals." A
beautiful thing begins to happen once a student
starts to recognize and utilize their own innate
strengths – they begin to believe in themselves.
When that belief in self becomes more and more
apparent, anything can be accomplished.

Motivating Your Inner Cheerleader

The nature of motivation is a funny thing. I
often find that people automatically assume that
some people just have it and some people don't.
However, motivation is no different than carrying
an empty bucket of water to a well. The people who
seem to be motivated have simply walked to the
well and filled their bucket. Motivation is not
something that we are automatically born with; it is
something that can and should always be cultivated.
If you feel like you lack motivation, you simply
haven't discovered that path to the well. Once you
filled your bucket, you'll find how easy it is to fill it
again and again and again.

In other words, knowing how your mind
operates will not only lead you down an easier path
to learning and applying new information, but it
will motivate you to do more and more. In fact, that
is largely what started the spark for Helen Keller.
Once Anne Sullivan, Heller's teacher, helped her
break through the isolation she felt by almost a
complete inability to understand and communicate
language, Helen had found her well and she
cultivated her motivation over and over again.

Try doing this exercise in order to begin finding your own internal cheerleader. Ask yourself – what gets you fired up? What gets you excited or passionate in general? Maybe it's a song for example (the *Rocky* theme song always does it for me), maybe it's a scene from a movie or TV show that you can repeatedly watch that raises emotions, or maybe it's a person or mentor in your life, maybe it's something in nature like a beautiful sunset, ocean waves rolling in or a hike through the woods. Perhaps it's a family member who may or may not be with us anymore. Yes, it could be competition as well, as long as you embrace the understanding that the ultimate purpose of competition is to bring out the best and get a better understanding of ourselves.

You probably didn't have to think long before coming up with a few things that get you fired up. You've just discovered your first, of many, wells. The great thing about it is you can keep going back to that well and will discover more and more wells as you do it. If a well dries up, which can happen because we are all constantly growing, learning, changing and evolving, then new ones can more easily be found. In other words, what fired you up today might not fire you up tomorrow and that's okay. **Think of motivation as a fluid, dynamic force that is constantly evolving, just as you are.**

In my 15-year teaching career, I've seen students gain motivational momentum to achieve complex tasks countless times. It happens in various forms – in the matter of minutes, over one class period or over the course of the school year. It continues to happen after students graduate and move onto college, a trade school or a profession and carries on into their adult lives. The times I've seen students gain that imperative momentum is always connected to the excitement they feel when accomplishing a task, large or small, by utilizing their full intellectual capacity.

And it's fun!

It's fun for anyone to see a learner find this excitement within themselves, not just for teachers. Yes, it's fun for me to see, in a physiology class for example, a student who first describes and comprehends pulmonary circulation. Or in biology class, when they break down and solve complex Hardy-Weinberg problems or apply the scientific method toward inquiry-based activities on science fair projects.

Even more rewarding, though, are how those experiences lead to the life achievements that lead these students down paths of continuous self-discovery, growth and passionate enjoyment in other people, in engineering, nature, politics, art, science, spirituality, athleticism and any, all and more of the latter.

The Classroom Setting

Unfortunately, all school systems (some more

than others) inadvertently take away one of a student's greatest natural strengths – their ability to utilize their innate selves for personal fulfillment and success. Schools don't do it on purpose. Teachers have a syllabus they need to follow with (hopefully diversified) quantitative assessment tools. Principals want to see rigorous learning happening in the classroom, which always seems to be action and goal oriented. In any given class, a percentage of a student's grade might depend on their performance on tests or quizzes, projects or papers, labs or homework, presentations or group work, etc., etc., etc. However, at what point did your class engage you in a deep level of contemplative self-analysis and exploration? What would that even look like inside a classroom? The only answer is, it would look different for every single student. While a student who is willing to learn can be facilitated to start self-analyzing, this type of work is most beneficial when done alone and might not be recognized in a classroom setting.

Imagine if a principal walked into a classroom and all students were spread out, within a few miles of each other. Some students were by themselves and some were in groups. Some students were painting in an art room, others were doing Tai Chi on the soccer field, a few more were singing and playing an instrument in the choir room and others were taking a nature walk outside. Everyone was doing something different with the sole purpose of "discovering" themselves and their inner strengths. While all those activities can be enlightening as you self-discover, it's very hard for an instructor to personalize that process for every student in a classroom.

A teacher can and should diversify the way they facilitate your learning, but it only scratches the surface compared to what you can do on your own.

Your job, as a student, is to bridge the gap between the classroom and your education by first recognizing yourself in that equation and then applying yourself in a way which utilizes your own personal strengths.

So, find your strengths. Once you do, personalize your learning style not just in the classroom, but to anywhere and anytime you want to gain further knowledge and insight. Once you're in the habit of tapping into your strengths, taking decisive, productive action becomes much easier.

MR. PFAFF'S TAKEAWAYS

- Recognize the multitude of ways in which you can be "smart."

- Identify your strongest personal "intelligences."

- Explore specific learning processes to unlock your potential.

- Find endless motivation within yourself by knowing yourself.

CHAPTER 4 Bloom's Taxonomy

"Knowing is not enough, we must apply. Willing is not enough, we must do."
— Bruce Lee, martial artist, actor

In 1956 an educational psychologist named Dr. Benjamin Bloom helped lead the development of a classification system to help promote higher forms of thinking. This is now known as Bloom's Taxonomy. It's often displayed in some sort of graphic organizer that lists a hierarchy of educational objectives from lowest to highest like the one below:

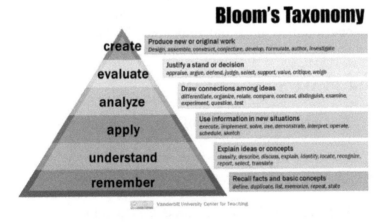

Bloom's Taxonomy

create — Produce new or original work
Design, assemble, construct, conjecture, develop, formulate, author, investigate

evaluate — Justify a stand or decision
appraise, argue, defend, judge, select, support, value, critique, weigh

analyze — Draw connections among ideas
differentiate, organize, relate, compare, contrast, distinguish, examine, experiment, question, test

apply — Use information in new situations
execute, implement, solve, use, demonstrate, interpret, operate, schedule, sketch

understand — Explain ideas or concepts
classify, describe, discuss, explain, identify, locate, recognize, report, select, translate

remember — Recall facts and basic concepts
define, duplicate, list, memorize, repeat, state

Vanderbilt University Center for Teaching

As you can see, the six levels range from the simple recall or recognition of facts, as the lowest level, through increasingly more complex and abstract mental levels, to the highest orders classified as evaluation and creation. In other words, "low" levels of learning include memorizing and remembering facts on any given concept while higher levels of learning and understanding include applying, analyzing and evaluating the information in that concept. And at the highest level, the learner creates new, original work.

Climbing The Pyramid

In my experience working with students over the years, I've discovered an inevitable truth as it relates to this idea – it's no fun to be at the bottom of the pyramid! Think about it. How much fun would you have, or more importantly, how much use would it serve if you had to memorize a bunch of facts about an event, whether it be in history, science or math, without seeing any real applications? If you had to recite those facts on a quiz or test, chances are you'd forget over half of it by the end of the day. So, what is the point? It's wasted lifetime.

While being able to recall facts in order to apply them is important, memorizing alone without seeing or discovering any real application is of little use. It's one thing to know that opposite charges attract each other in science, and it's another thing to create a project that illustrates it or find a useful purpose. It's one thing to memorize that a circuit is a pathway that electrons follow, and it's another thing to create a working circuit yourself in robotics. It's one thing to know the combatants, dates and political leaders involved in World War II, and it's another thing to perform in a play that takes place during the political, economic, and social times in which it occurred.

Think of a song, dance move or video game you've mastered. Isn't it fun to apply the song you know by singing it with a friend to make them smile, or perform that dance move at a party or rip your opponent's skull and vertebrae clean off their body during a fatality move in Mortal Kombat? Of course, it is! However, just like all students' minds are different, so are all teachers' minds.

Different Teaching Styles

Not all teachers possess and/or employ pedagogical strategies that favor your own personal intelligences. You'll see diversification of curriculum, to different degrees, depending on which classroom you're in. Teachers are all so different because personalities are all so different and teaching itself is very much an extension of one's own personality.

That being said, here's the trick: **You still have control over how you learn and educate yourself in any particular class.** You can control that variable and make it constant in any class by taking responsibility for how you apply the information you're receiving. **The difference is you have to make a habit of looking for ways to apply,**

evaluate and analyze the information you're receiving on your own if it's not being supplied to you.

In fact, you should be in the habit of doing this on your own even when applications are supplied to you by your teacher, to help internalize information further. When you do this, you start stimulating other areas of your brain besides the area in your frontal lobe, which is responsible for short term or "working" memory.

Finding Your Application

Don't limit your definition of the word "apply." Forms of application can occur in your own mind as you hear and receive information. For instance, if you hear new information in any particular class and link it to information you already knew in the past, you are applying. If you find symbolism or an analogy which is specific to you, you are applying. If you form questions on how this information might be relevant in new situations, you are applying.

When you seek ways to apply, either in your own mind or through actions, you are stimulating other areas of the brain to share the work that is being placed on your frontal lobe. Information becomes easier to retain because you're transferring it to other areas of your brain, such as the hippocampus, which is responsible for long term memory. It's almost like recruiting some friends to help you with a monotonous task such as digging a deep hole in the ground. With only one shovel and all alone, digging that hole will take a long time and you'll get tired quickly. You might even give up. However, with three other friends helping and cracking jokes as you all shovel, not only will the job be easier and quicker, but it will most likely be more enjoyable as well. Examples of how this applies (pun intended) when you receive new information does not need to be complex in the least.

In physiology, for example, we discuss different types of bone breaks when discussing the skeletal system. Most students have never heard of a greenstick fracture before, which often occurs during childhood when bones are still soft and haven't fully developed or ossified. It's a type of break that bends on one side of the bone but only frays on the other. If students did nothing more than listen to this information, chances are they might forget what type of break it was by the next class because their frontal lobe didn't recruit any help. However, if someone, either the teacher or the student, applies it to another situation, especially a situation they already know, it becomes very easy to recall.

To facilitate this process with that particular example, I refer to any time my students might have seen a young child sitting or playing. I'll then prompt them to think about how effortlessly flexible and limber those kids are while they're having fun.

You might see children sitting in some awkward position with their legs bent back while watching TV, tumble rolling over their heads or doing backbends. I'll prompt my students further and ask them to imagine an older adult, such as their grandparent, trying to pull off the same thing. Inevitably my students laugh at the thought. Then, I begin to connect that idea to the skeletal system, because it's the same way in its limber flexibility. I simply took information they already knew, which was a child's natural flexible state, and linked it to new information they received, a greenstick fracture. As a result, the hippocampus shares in the work.

However, say I didn't give that example in class. Then students must recognize that it's their opportunity to seek their own application to make their own learning easier, as well as more fun. In that same example, maybe a student might think of a tree branch since it's called a "greenstick" fracture and create an analogy between that kind of bone break and a branch on a tree that's still growing, fresh with green leaves, and very flexible. They might think further to an old, dead tree branch and how brittle it is and how easily it could be broken. In either case, whether the application is teacher driven or student driven, the mind can easily recall and make sense of that new information.

Try this exercise, take a random, unknown fact that you will hear or see today (new information is constantly coming at us every day) and try to link it to your long-term memory by connecting it to something you already know in your own mind. Once you've done that, think of some ways in which you might be able to apply that information. Once you've done that, you can let it go and stop thinking about it. Chances are you'll find you can still recall that random fact even days later because it is now part of your permanent knowledge. The same technique can be used in and out of the classroom.

MR. PFAFF'S TAKEAWAYS

- Apply and analyze all new information you receive to understand it better.

- Connect new ideas to things you already know.

- Have more fun while learning by taking initiative to exercise your higher order thinking skills.

CHAPTER 5 Kinesthetic Intelligence

"Children learn as they play. Most importantly, in play children learn how to learn."
                              – O. Fred Donaldson, Ph. D., play
                                                        specialist

Have you ever observed a child while they are playing? The power of their imagination can literally take over the room, no matter what they are doing. Concentration seems effortless and they are completely engrossed and alive in whatever fantasy they're engaged in for that moment. Even more impressive is a child's ability to slip in and out of their own fantasy as they move around dolls, toy trucks, or even a stick they found on the ground. In one moment, they can be in their own fantasy flying through space, shooting lasers out of the eyes of a figurine they're holding to defend earth against alien invaders, and a split second later they'll answer their mom who just told them dinner is ready. Then they slip right back into the "game!"

Kinesthetic Play

The level of involvement a child has during play stimulates intrapersonal imagination, kinesthetic application, visual manipulation of tactile objects, and interpersonal collaboration with others. And this mentions just a few areas that their own personal brain recruits. We can learn a lot by watching kids.

Even if your self-assessment test revealed a low kinesthetic score of intelligence, or you personally consider yourself to be weak in this particular area, it doesn't mean that this gateway isn't a rich, valuable resource for you to engage in meaningful, deep levels of learning and comprehension. The opportunities to leverage the broad area of pedagogical kinesthetic tools are endless.

Movement

How exactly does kinesthetic intelligence work?

Whether you're building, acting, dancing, touching, or playing, the common thread is that you are moving. My Bachelors of Science degree in Kinesiology, the movement sciences, from Penn State University, coupled with my Masters of Education, along with years of teaching, opened my eyes to the powerful gateway that movement plays in all levels of learning. In fact, the only way to make use of any kind of information or idea is to move and act on it. You don't need to be an athlete to capitalize in this area, you simply need to use your vessel that your brain controls as a gateway to learn.

In terms of your education, let's look at how our brains remember information, based on numerous studies on memory. As an example, let's explore an actor's ability to remember lines. Think about the challenge actors have, particularly in live theatre. Not only are actors required to remember many pages of dialogue within a play containing long monologues and complex language, but they also have to remember where and when to move. That's not even mentioning the myriad of emotions and feelings within the character they're portraying that ultimately comes together to move an audience. The easiest way for actors to do it, even from a play they've performed a year prior, is to accompany their lines of dialog with movement, intention and context.

In 2008, England's Royal Shakespeare Company recruited 30 actors, in multiple roles, to stage all of Shakespeare's historical plays. All of them. That's *King John, Richard II, Henry IV Parts 1 and II, Henry V, Henry VI Parts I, II* and *III, Richard III* and *Henry VIII*. That's five generations of medieval power struggles (and you thought *Game of Thrones* was elaborate!) The actors had to remember thousands of lines and cues. Just to make things more challenging, Michael Boyd, the director of the company, decided to bring back four different plays the actors had done a year earlier at the same time.

Needless to say, the actors went into an anxiety-driven overload trying to remember lines and cues. For a short period, it appeared the actors would not be able to pull it off, until Boyd had the actors move by staging the scenes with no props, sets or costumes. All of a sudden, lines and cues previously forgotten were recalled with surprising ease. The physical act of the blocking and hitting marks helped stimulate the recall of those lines. In fact, the actors all knew exactly what to say when they were required to move with intention. Boyd said those "broken bits of memory" were brought back to life through the performance of the play. To top it off, anxiety levels went down among all the actors, not to mention that they started having a lot more fun.

There is a reason we call it a "play" and not a "work."

Remember the old saying, "It's not whether you win or lose, but how you play that is important"? Well, as a student, that old saying still applies – as long as you know how to play and the rules involved.

Physical movement, especially with intention behind it, could help you recall pieces of information you once heard, but assumed you had forgotten. It can also give meaning connected to that information, which makes it easier for you to apply, thus pushing you higher up Bloom's Taxonomy. What a powerful tool constantly available at your own moving fingertips!

What's In A Kinesthetic Name?

Let's start with a scenario and exercise to illustrate how a kinesthetic technique can be applied. Pretend you have just moved and are a freshman at a brand new high school and do not know a single person at the entire school! It's the first day of school and you're in your very first class of the day and find yourself in a large classroom with 30 other students. If this hypothetical scenario isn't already causing some anxiety, let's say your teacher says to the whole class that it's a requirement for everyone in the class to know every single student's name by the end of class, which is a 45-minute block of time.

While a lot of the other students might already know each other, you are in a room full of complete strangers. How successful do you think you would be at this task if the first student in the first row said their name, then moved onto the next, and the next, up and down the rows until the very last student? Unless you had a uniquely powerful photographic memory, chances are you'd remember less than a third of the names of your new peers.

Now, let's change the tool being used to accomplish this task. You and all the other students in the class are now required to stand up, walk around the classroom and say good morning to every single person as you pass them, while also shaking their hand and making eye contact. Then, all 30 students are required to continue standing and create a large circle in the middle of the room. The first student who says their name is now required to incorporate some sort of physical action and inflexion when they say it, which they feel captures the "essence" of their personality. After they do it, everyone in the circle is required to repeat the physical action and inflexion as they say that person's name. The action doesn't have to be elaborate and the essence of your personality could change from minute to minute depending on how you feel in that moment. Whatever action a student chooses in that moment is the right one and could be trusted.

Your own job is to trust whatever you're feeling in that moment when it's your turn. The action could be a shy wave, a salute, or a two- fisted King Kong style banging on the chest as you say your name.

One by one, each student begins to say their name with whatever inflection and movement comes to mind. One by one, the whole class repeats the name with the inflexion, movement (often with a laugh) until you get to the very last student. The exercise is repeated around the circle a few times until the teacher asks for a brave volunteer to attempt to go around the room and recall the name and physical action of each student in the class. A courageous student (my intention and hope are that by the end of this book, that student will be you), who didn't know one person's name before entering the class that day, raises their hand and decides to give it a shot. Chances are very high you'd get through almost everyone on your first attempt. Even if you didn't, let's say you got through six students and were stuck on that seventh student's uncommon name. Chances are very high that when the particular student shows you the physical movement that accompanies the name, it will trigger your memory and you will be able to recall it and continue around the circle. Even if you don't remember that student's name, the physical movement, eye contact and temporary connection with that new student uses a kinesthetic technique to tap into additional devices such as interpersonal, linguistic, musical, and visual/spatial learning.

In other words, you asked different areas of your brain, each containing different strengths, to help you accomplish a task. So, if they have to tell you their name, I can guarantee you won't forget it after that. In addition, chances are even higher that you remembered a bit about the essence of that person. In other words, you had more of an understanding about them. Lastly, it's almost certain that you smiled and had some fun, even if it was a bit scary at first.

Personally, I have done that very exercise with thousands of students in my classes over the years and have literally seen the culture and climate of the room change. A sense of joy replaces anxiety and starts to fill the room as hearts and minds of students begin to open more, and miraculously, remember more. After about 10 minutes of this simple exercise, I have seen, over and over again, almost 99% of my students successfully recall the names and movements of all their peers even if they were brand new to the school. In addition, they also have a small glimpse into the personality of their peers, not to mention they had fun.

Why should your learning of any other new material be any different? Isn't it more enjoyable and successful to recruit "friends," whether figuratively in your own brain or literally in the whole class, to accomplish any task? By incorporating that child-like sense of kinesthetic play and imagination, you'd be amazed what kind of complex tasks you're capable of, what you've always been capable of since you were a toddler. The greatest part of all is that you alone have the power to facilitate this action at any time and with any task. You do not need a teacher to employ this strategy; you only need the knowledge of the tool and the initiative to use it.

All Hands On Deck

Memory recall with actors isn't the only way kinesthetic techniques could be useful. Any opportunity to get a "hands on" experience, whether it's measuring or weighing in science, learning a new dance move with a partner, or changing spark plugs under the hood of a car involves some sort of tactile activity. So much information can be gained, used and applied when we use our manual dexterity and the sense of touch in some way. In fact, with practice, using tactile feedback can give you an enormous advantage over others, regardless of who's higher in kinesthetic intelligence.

Ever see one of those blind-folded martial artists who seem to have a sixth sense of what's happening around them? How do they know when and where to move? When it comes to using tactile information to learn, use and experience benefit, Bruce Lee is a phenomenal example.

Before Bruce Lee developed his own style of Martial Arts known as Jeet Kune Do (JKD), he studied a form of Chinese Martial Art known as Wing Chun Kung Fu. I've been studying Wing Chun Kung Fu for over a year now, and one of the training techniques in it is called, "Chi Sao," which literally means "sticky hands." In this technique, practitioners connect arms with another partner and use sensory information from their opponent to take control of the centerline, the most optimal fighting position. They do this using the sense of touch.

As a result of this information, they can interpret and react to an opponent appropriately due to the contact they have with their opponent's arms or other parts of their body, such as the legs ("Chi Gerk"). In other words, instead of using visual or verbal cues that an opponent might be trying to flip, punch or kick them, they use tactile information. This tactile, kinesthetic practice technique can even translate to fighting situations before they're in contact with an opponent because they constantly move to bridge that distance gap with their arms and legs, almost like an insect with antennas, to make the contact. Whether their opponent is attacking or retreating, punching or blocking, striking or grappling, they can gain information, even without the use of their vision, and calmly react appropriately.

I wish I could say this technique is easy, but as a lifelong learner, I will be continuing to study to improve at this technique. The point is, **you gain considerable knowledge through touch** and any opportunity to use your own body, your vessel to learn, could be useful.

For example, do you tend to get nervous before written assessments or presentations in class? Techniques such as "progressive relaxation" actually uses the body to help calm muscles and eventually center the mind. It starts with doing a self-analysis of where your muscles might be tense, perhaps in your shoulders or lower in your stomach. Then you systematically move through the body from toe to head, contracting and relaxing various muscle groups. As a result, you put your body in a more relaxed state which has a calming effect on the mind. When the mind is relaxed and centered, you can think more clearly.

There are lots of ways to center your mind, and the mind does control the body, not the other way around. Contracting a muscle to begin with originates from a nerve impulse that comes from the mind. The kinesthetic technique of using your mind to calm your body can put you in a more relaxed state to recall and apply information in a clear, concise manner.

MR. PFAFF'S TAKEAWAYS

- Use various forms of movement to stimulate learning and activate memory.

- Explore with your hands to gain more information.

- Playing and having fun also equates to powerful learning.

CHAPTER 6 Interpersonal Intelligence

"Best way to sell something: don't sell anything. Earn the awareness, respect, and trust of those who might buy."
            – Rand Fishkin, CEO and founder,
                                SEOmoz

We all know that kind of student or friend who seems to be a natural born salesman or leader. They are the "take charge" type, especially during group work and social situations where they are great at getting others to work together cooperatively. **They are out going, always seem to know the best way or time to approach people, and seem to bring a group together.**

Everyone seems to want to work with them as well. Students of this "type" have a high probability of moving into leadership roles such as class president, team captain, teacher's assistant or simply, they might sell ever single candy bar needed to raise money for the school play. Massive undertakings can often be achieved through their skill in fostering group effort.

And then there's the student in class who can't stop making you laugh. We've all been there, myself included. In fact, chances are very high that the student who is making you laugh is also making other students in the class laugh because they're funny, overly sociable and cleverly out going.

Whether it was appropriate or not, that same "type" seems to have a magnetism when it comes to attracting attention. Even if they do get in trouble with a teacher, or any authority figure for that matter, for causing too much distraction, they seem to have a talent for talking their way out of it, or at least, they can lighten the mood.

I have sometimes seen this type of student get mislabeled as a "class clown" if they become overly distracting. While they might face some challenges such as missing pertinent details delivered by an instructor, they are not very different from the first type of student described. The only difference is they have an undirected mind that can cause them to lose sight of what's important, such as the information being delivered in class. How can they hear the important stuff? They're too busy making you laugh!

The negative result to this type can be missed deadlines on assignments, lower quiz and test scores, and a compromised grade. But by self-recognizing and self-directing their strengths, which again is part of the on-going process of education (not schooling), they will experience the same kind of success as the first type of student described.

So, if you scored high or just know you are high in this particular aptitude, listen carefully.

Whether you fall into the former or latter student type, you have a high aptitude for interpersonal intelligence and are extremely capable of blossoming into a very successful, rewarding, useful (and often lucrative) career working with others.

People with a high aptitude for interpersonal intelligence are great at reading both verbal and nonverbal cues from others. They not only interact with others with ease, but they almost seem to "get" people. They're good at sensing the moods of others and even an entire room. Very often you might call this type of person for advice, especially when it comes to relationships.

While people with this kind of intelligence might steer toward professions as politicians, actors, teachers and social workers, they can also be highly skilled poker players or criminal profilers for the FBI because to be good at those professions, you have to be good at reading people. But you don't have to be a master poker player and "reader of the tell," like the poker great Johnny Chan, to utilize this intelligence method to find avenues and nuances toward deep learning and understanding. We all have the ability to read others.

In fact, one of the distinct advantages, which ensured the evolution and survival of the human race, is our ability to recognize the faces and expressions of other human beings. The innate ability that humans and monkeys have to determine friend from foe is so important for survival that our brains evolved to store this complex capability in our temporal lobe. Once again, we've found another friend, in a distinct location in our brain, holding a shovel, willing to help us dig that ditch.

On an even deeper level, we all have the instinctual need to connect with and socialize with others. It's the reason why huge efforts have been made to eliminate the use of solitary confinement in prison systems because that practice defies what it means to be human! So now that we know we all possess an innate level of interpersonal intelligence to varying degrees, let's focus on how we can use it, capitalize on it, and share it with our peers.

Peer Tutoring And Cooperative Learning

A powerful pedagogical tool, from which I have seen countless students achieve high levels of success both in and outside the classroom, is the use of peer tutoring and cooperative learning. Peer tutoring means exactly what it sounds like – using your peers, classmates and friends to help you understand.

Have you ever noticed that sometimes you just grasp an idea better if it's explained to you by a friend, rather than a teacher? Maybe the teacher was using language or terminology that didn't resonate with you when they explained it or perhaps they weren't using examples relevant to your own social world. However, when a friend is explaining it, especially someone who knows you well, they seem to be able to get you to understand despite the fact that their content knowledge might not be as extensive as that of your teacher. You don't need to score high in the interpersonal intelligence category to use this method of learning; you simply have to take initiative.

Why does it work? First off, let's state the obvious: you can save face with a friend. If you're having a discussion with another friend, you're probably not as worried about exposing what you don't know, or what you didn't do, so you're more relaxed. Even if you're formally exercising this process in class and have paired up with a classmate you don't know very well, you're still probably more relaxed than in a larger group situation and in front of the teacher. As a result, a sense of freedom to take chances happens and this stimulates a faster learning curve within you.

It obviously helps when one person in the group has more knowledge to share than the other, but the other person does not need to be an "expert." In fact, you'll find that more learning ultimately takes place from the questions that arise from peer tutoring conversations than the factual answers themselves.

Whether you're using this technique inside the class, in the locker room or on the school bus, do not accept "pecking order." Pairing up with someone or others who are performing higher or lower is more effective with this technique because it does set up the lower performer to get up to speed quickly. However, the lower performer in one particular unit, concept or problem is often the higher performer on the next, so do not accept the constant role of only "tutee" or "tutor." The process of peer tutoring doesn't necessarily have more benefit for the student tutee either.

Have you ever noticed that if you have to explain something to another person, you are able to understand and internalize the information on a deeper level yourself? You might notice that as you're explaining ideas, you self-discover, in that moment, where some of your own misconceptions lie. That discovery might prompt you to seek and research the answers to your own questions so you can explain it better to your peer, which only deepens and clarifies your own content knowledge. Make no mistake that both people in this peer process benefit enormously.

Peer tutoring also serves as a valuable tool for teachers to uncover where misconceptions might lie, which they can then address later in the class. The process also empowers students to more accurately self-recognize what they know and what they don't know. It builds confidence with both the tutee and tutor because when they finish the exercise they are excited to share what they've learned or have insightful questions which deepens their own knowledge.

While peer tutoring can be extremely effective in all kinds of settings, I've found that, whether you're a student, teacher or administrator, certain ground rules should be set to reap the most benefits with the time you have, especially if you're doing it in a class setting.

- **Access the knowledge:** I first start with a list of the concepts or problems you are responsible for knowing and have you quickly and quantifiably rate your knowledge on a scale from 1-5 for each one. Examples of concepts might be the details responsible for Replication, Transcription and Translation within DNA, Hardy Weinberg problems in Evolution, or Dihybrid, Sex Linked, Blood-Type, and Incomplete/Co-Dominant Punnett Square problems in Genetics.

- **Pair the students:** For each concept, I break you and your peers up according to your own self-assessment rating. I pair students who scored themselves lower (a 1 or 2) with students who scored themselves higher (a 4 or 5). Obviously, logistical problems arise if a you and a lot of your peers have rated yourselves as a 3, or if most students are skewed to one side. At that point, I might pair you up in small cooperative groups instead, such as pairing one of the few students who self-rated themselves high with three or four students who had a lower self-rating. The pairing of the groups isn't as important as the process of pairing you up with a peer and having a focused discussion on the content or problem. I'll separate you and your partner(s) into private discussion pods both in and outside the classroom and will set a time limit for each concept.

- **Switch it up:** If you were the peer tutee and have been working with the peer tutor for a while, I'll switch the roles in the group and have you play the role of tutor and try to correctly do a problem or explain a concept back to the tutee.

- **Reconvene:** Once the time limit for your small group conversation has ended, we all reconvene into a large class group again and I ask questions to the class. Invariably, just as many hands that originally self-rated themselves low in comprehension are raised to answer summary questions as those who self-rated themselves high.

- **Move on:** We then go onto the next concept and the pairing of groups often changes because areas of knowledge range from topic to topic, so the tutee in the last break out session is often the tutor in the next. The learning curve that can happen within a single class when using this process is remarkable.

A Preview Of Difficult Subjects

Discussing content-driven material that you are hearing for the first time can often be overwhelming, particularly in science and history where you're learning new terms that can sound like a foreign language! So, here's a learning tool I like to use in my honors and regular biology classes when we are discussing challenging content that you haven't been exposed to a lot prior to our course. Examples include concepts in cellular respiration, photosynthesis, DNA replication, transcription, translation and genetics. So how can you make sense of all these new terms and information?

The first trick is to make sure it's actually not the first time you hear about these concepts, so I give you a preview. (I'll discuss this in-depth in a later chapter covering "Habits of Work and Mind.") Any kind of preview of the material beforehand, if only for 5-10 minutes, is extremely helpful not only for comprehension, but for confidence. And in the long run, it actually saves time because you process the lesson in class as you're experiencing it a lot quicker having some prior knowledge, even if it's limited.

When students come into the process with some of their own questions, with loose connections to past knowledge, and with ideas of their own, it makes for a much more active, receptive learner, especially when the student is receiving relatively new information. And even if you literally just heard something you've never heard before, talking it over with a friend can be of enormous benefit.

Role Playing

Role playing and simulations are powerful gateways to stimulate your brain as well. In history for example, playing the role of a historic figure you're studying can give you an unforgettable learning experience to truly internalize the motives, beliefs and actions of a character, in addition to the social, religious, political and economic times in which he or she lived. Role playing to get a glimpse into your character over the course of one class is obviously less time consuming than putting on a play that requires months of rehearsal and numerous performances, but is still of great benefit. Depending on how far you go with the role-playing process, it could inform and educate on such an internal level that it might even change your perspective or the way you see the world.

James Cromwell, for example, the actor from the movie *Babe*, felt an internal calling to become a vegan and join animal activist groups, resulting in his willingness to get arrested in protests to protect our environment and animals, as a result of playing the role of "Farmer Hoggett" in that film. To say he exemplified a deep understanding and empathy for animals, particularly pigs, after role playing is an understatement.

Simulations

Simulations, especially in science, technology, engineering, and the arts, are another extremely powerful tool to engage and inspire learners of all types. This is especially true if you experience high learning outcomes from various forms of interaction.

A simulation is literally defined as "any imitation of a situation or process." There are endless opportunities and ways to set up an interactive situation that imitates a process such as exams, emergencies within a lab, sports, etc. The point is to get the experience of the process by interacting with it, in some way, before it actually takes place.

If you're reading this book, you might have already tried a simulation in some way shape or form. Testing, particularly on standardized tests like the SAT or AP Exam, is a common example. On standardized tests such as these, the challenge for you is that it's an experience you've never had before, not to mention it's partially a test in "test taking" itself.

So how do you get good at it? Practice through simulation. You could easily access or create your own practice questions and take a self-administered exam by setting a timer and following all testing protocols, which are easily found online for standardized tests. The "interpersonal" part of this process is the fact that you're setting up a simulation with the environment that will help prepare you for the real deal.

Virtual Reality

Innovators in technology have taken the process of simulation to a whole new level with the use of Virtual Reality (VR) devices. You've all seen these devices before in some way, shape or form. Just picture a large binocular style pair of glasses that fit over your eyes. While it might feel awkward having a piece of clunky plastic and metal strapped around your head at first, that will be forgotten within a split second once it's turned on. These simulations are extremely fun, engaging and personally interactive.

Keeping up with best teaching practices, particularly in science, technology, engineering, math and the arts, has provided me with the benefit of seeing some really cool stuff. Last year, I had my own personal demonstration of a few of the latest VR devices on the market. My very first experience was a simulation in which I was traveling through a blood vessel of the circulatory system of a human being, as if I were a drop of blood plasma! Writing about the experience won't do it justice, unless of course, you're more of a logical/mathematical learner, but I'll try. Picture a real-life version of *Fantastic Voyage*, the 1966 epic about a submarine crew that was shrunk down to microscopic size to travel through the body of a scientist to treat his inured brain. I literally had the sensation that I was on that voyage traveling in the blood stream within an artery. Everywhere I looked I would see and hear something different. Next to me was a red blood cell attached to some oxygen, up ahead I saw white blood cells fighting various bacteria, viruses and germs, down below I could see platelets in the form of cell fragments helping to clot blood at the site of a puncture wound. I could hear the beating of the heart as it forcefully propelled me forward down the vessel.

That simulation only scratches the surface of the capabilities of a VR device. You can build your own models with different painting and drawing features, create holographic images (I placed a skeleton next to a colleague, for example) or choose various art galleries to explore for a very personalized experience. It's so interactive that you can inspect various paintings and sculptures, of your choice, from different self-chosen angles and select specific audio that only you'd like to hear.

This year, I'm already using it in our class to show my physiology students three dimensional, close-up views of all the various human organs within different systems and how they interact with each other. I'm able to pull individual organs out, rotate them or the whole organism itself, layer different organ systems, trigger movements, etc. The technology has endless potential. In fact, I believe in ten years VR devices will be as common in classrooms as laptops are today. However, you don't need a fancy VR device to experience the benefits of simulation because the power of your imagination to set up an interactive experience with the environment will always be your most powerful tool.

The Creative Gift

If you're one of those students who have discovered you are high in this particular intelligence with a very creative imagination, but often feel you get distracted by your peers or your environment in some way, remember that you are dealing with a gift, not a curse! If you have difficulty concentrating in class and overly socialize, then try to hone your ability to self-direct your focus onto the content within a social context. Any way in which you can interact, even if it's a prop for a role or part for a supply, sharpens this faculty.

Try, also, to participate in other school settings outside the classroom such as writing for your school paper, or get involved in your church, home or sport community to tap into, test and direct your natural strength. If you're still not convinced that you are sitting on a powerful educational tool at your fingertips, here are just a few of many examples I experienced personally in my own classroom.

The At-Risk Students

During my first few years teaching at South Boston High School I had two students that any educator would consider "at risk." One student (let's call him Brad) was on the borderline of dropping out of high school altogether. He had failing grades in almost all his classes and seemed completely disinterested in anything being taught in every one of his courses. But he was never disinterested when it came to hanging out with friends and he always had a loyal group of friends who inherently seemed to trust and confide in him at all times.

One day, Brad told me he was going to drop out of school. We had a long talk which mostly consisted of me begging him to stay in school. Thank goodness he did. Brad finally graduated by the skin of his teeth, but with no plans for college or any further schooling. We lost touch after he finished high school.

Years later, however, after I had left teaching at South Boston High School to move to Los Angeles to pursue acting, I received a personal Facebook message from Brad. He thanked me for what I did for him in high school and said he wanted to get into the entertainment business as an actor, writer and director and was looking to move to LA.

As we spoke this time, I noticed something different about him. He was passionate, energetic, focused and excited. Brad had found and tapped into his interpersonal intelligence. Brad was a sponge for information as I shared everything with him that I knew about the business. Contrary to the student I knew in high school, this time he took all my advice. It was clear to me that even though his schooling ended after high school, his education did not.

When Brad first got to LA, I brought him onto a few different sets I was working on. As expected, he immediately hit it off with the crew and cast. I introduced him to some business partners and he started collaborating with them, helping to produce demo reels, web series and short films. Over a short period of time, he developed an entourage of industry professionals to collaborate with regularly. Now, he is making a living at directing his own independent feature films that get great distribution deals.

Brad's interpersonal intelligence has allowed him to become successful because the whole business is based on working together with other creatives and business professionals. I've seen him on various sets many times and he has a strong, natural ability at collaborating, motivating and utilizing others. Brad's already found success in a very competitive industry despite the fact that schooling was never his thing.

Another student (let's call him Randy) was very similar in some ways, but different in others. He didn't want to drop out of high school, but he definitely had a difficult time concentrating in class. Randy was always telling jokes, stories and laughing with his friends with absolutely no focus on any kind of task he was responsible for in or out of class. He didn't take redirection very well and was often in trouble for distracting others. As a result, his grades suffered due to distraction and he spent a good amount of time in my class after school where we had countless discussions about developing his ability to focus.

All of the faculty loved Randy, especially me. He was so personable, out-going, warm, friendly and extremely funny. One day we were having one of our many after-school conversations and I told him he should consider a career in sales after he finished school. I explained why by pointing out his interpersonal strengths. At the time, I wasn't sure if my words registered. As an educator, you don't always get to see the results of the work you do with students. However, with him, I did. Last year he posted a message on my Facebook wall saying, "Mr. Pfaff, years ago you said to me, 'Randy – you should go into sales.' Ten years later I'm head of my sales team at AT&T. Thanks."

As an educator, you live for moments like that. It's why teaching is one of the most rewarding professions one could have. But what Randy and

Brad said and did didn't surprise me. Their innate interpersonal intelligence was always there. They just needed some time and direction to learn how to tap into it.

You, too, can tap into, direct and use your strong social style to learn and accomplish anything. Teamwork will always be a part of any kind of work you pursue. As an interpersonal learner, you're already a natural at it. You just have to understand that in addition to being fun, it could be of extreme educational value. Use your peers, friends, family and colleagues to bounce ideas off of and work through problems. Discussing ideas in groups will open yourself up to different perspectives expanding your mind. The potential of you combined with the surrounding community is limitless. Learning doesn't have to be hard and the irony of the powerful phrase, "we can work it out" can only by discovered by knowing yourself.

MR. PFAFF'S TAKEAWAYS

- Create structured study time with friends, peers and colleagues to learn more easily.

- Initiate content specific conversations with others to process information.

- Role play, create simulations and Facetime chat when you can't meet in person.

CHAPTER 7 Visual-Spatial Intelligence

"Whatever great things we build, end up building us"

> *– Jim Rohn, an American entrepreneur,*
> *author and motivational speaker*

The world's greatest engineers, architects, physicists, police detectives and graphic designers are off the charts in this particular intelligence. Visual-spatial learners tend to think in pictures rather than verbal description and understand things as a whole instead of a part or sequence.

While visual and spatial ability are both used to navigate, fix, measure, create and understand, I find it useful to draw distinctions between the two in terms of your learning. Understanding the differences will empower you to use specific strategies that have specific benefits and potential.

Spatial Intelligence

In 2010, *Scientific American* magazine published a fascinating article about a challenging IQ test that was administered to thousands of students in California in 1920 by Lewis Terman, a psychologist from Stanford University. The IQ test was rigorously designed and used to measure the same things that most IQ and similar tests do today – to identify intelligence.

So why was *Scientific American* writing an article about something that happened almost a century ago? Because the IQ test, as with many others, failed to identify intelligence in several specific, important areas. This resulted in not recognizing the intelligence of two of the world's greatest inventors. According to Terman's IQ test, Luis Walter Alvarez and William Shockley, were two typical students without any exceptional capabilities. However, years later after taking Terman's IQ test, both Luis Alvarez and William Shockley went on to win a Nobel Prize!

Clearly Terman's IQ test missed something. That test, as with many of its kind, unfortunately failed to recognize Spatial Intelligence.

Standardized Tests

Standardized tests are meant to measure specific verbal, reading and math skills you learned in school, and they can fall short. Little attention on these tests or in traditional classrooms is spent on identifying the kind of student who likes to build and work with their hands, or tinker with tangible objects, or find ways to repair things. I've seen too many students of this type become disinterested in school and in worst-case scenarios, drop out of the educational mindset and school system altogether. It's these individuals who have the strongest potential to build, repair and tinker with microchips, molecules and electrons later in life!

Even if your school lacks outlets such as a Maker's lab, robotics team, or exams that effectively empower this particular faculty, do not get discouraged. Instead, get encouraged knowing you have discovered this strength in yourself. Don't allow any kind of written test that you take in your lifetime define what you're capable of. Written tests will ALWAYS fall short in this prediction of your potential.

The true determinant of success is mustering the courage and grit to analyze yourself, to find your own strengths, and to put those strengths into action. I'm pretty sure somewhere in the world, *MacGyver* is smiling at that fact. (By the way, the remake of this TV series is just as fun as the classic.)

Within my own personal experiences, I've seen countless examples of people who exhibit the innate strength to self-analyze. I'm sure after reading a few of these examples, you'll realize you do as well.

After I graduated high school, I could barely contain the excitement I felt as I began my freshmen year at Penn State University and moved into my first official home away from home, my dorm room. Dorm rooms were small (and probably still are!), about 12 feet by 13 feet, and the University already had a basic design laid out before anyone moved in – two beds perpendicular to each other against adjacent walls, two desks next to each other against another wall, and a window on the far wall. Each bed had its own small storage shelf/cabinet and closet next to it. Not knowing any better, my roommate and I just chose a bed and unpacked. That's all there was to it right? Not exactly.

Individualized Decor

We lived in an athlete's dorm building with mostly football, baseball and track athletes. Then we met two cool guys who lived down the hall from us who didn't play sports at all. I was never quite sure how they got into that particular dorm building. What I do remember, though, is their dorm room. While they had the same exact size and floor layout as we did, their dorm room looked entirely different. They had literally transformed that small dorm room into the coolest, most efficiently used space I had ever seen.

They purchased chains, removed the legs of their beds, and actually lifted the beds up off the floor so that one long side of the bed was resting on top of the shelving unit and the other side of the bed was held up by chains attached to that same wall, army bunker style. Now that they had all that space underneath both beds, they arranged a futon couch, mini fridge, and stereo system under one bed and a small black couch with side end tables under the other. They installed mini shelving units next to a TV on the far side of the wall which had books, CDs, movies and pictures neatly organized on them. They laid out a gorgeous carpet that was measured, cut and fit to the exact floor dimensions of the room, so they had wall-to-wall carpeting. On the walls, they installed mirrors that made the dorm space look even bigger. In addition, they even changed the color of the light bulbs in their room to blue for this cool, Zen feeling. Their room, because it was decorated to the nines, became the primary place to hang out on the whole floor.

When I reflect on those fun college days, it doesn't surprise me to recall that one of those guys was an engineering major. His natural faculty with spatial intelligence was remarkable. At the time, I did realize how talented he was in that particular area within the first week we met, but as our friendship grew, it became even more apparent. He had a collection of different sized Rubik cubes on his shelves that he could solve in front of you with astonishing speed.

This guy had to build a mini catapult for one of his engineering classes and calculate where the launched marbles would land. He had so much fun doing that project that he just continued building them for fun. It always amazed me that he would estimate distances, while converting units in his head, with astonishing accuracy. I'm not sure where he is today, but I'm confident he's extremely successful in his field and in life, because even back then he was particularly self-aware – not only of his own innate strengths but how to apply them.

Pictionary Perfect

I have an older cousin from Chicago who was never very crazy about school when he was growing up. It just didn't engage him. We'd see each other once a year in the summer for a few weeks at the beach in Rockaway Point, New York, and while he would tell me about lots of things going on in his life, school wasn't one of them. Other things, such as drawing, assembling and dissembling model cars, boats, watches and kicking all our asses in Pictionary were more his thing. Anything you wanted to see on paper he could sketch for you from memory or imagination with amazing visual accuracy.

However, since he wasn't very motivated by anything he was doing at school, he received below average grades in both middle and high school and decided not to pursue further schooling after high school. Instead, he went to work for a moving company. While I didn't personally know the teachers, pedagogical philosophies and structure of the schools he attended, I'd bet that a predominant part of the education he received at those schools didn't empower him to utilize or tap into those innate strengths he had with spatial intelligence.

Thank God, my cousin never let his schooling get in the way of his education. After many years of working for a moving company and a lot of self-reflection, he decided to do the prerequisite work needed to apply to architecture school. Eventually, he was accepted into architecture school and he had a much different outlook and result with the work.

Here, because he was keenly aware of his own strengths and was given many opportunities to apply them, he had a lot more fun, graduated at the top of his class, and is now working for a very successful architecture company. As a very talented architect, he plans on opening up his own firm in a few years.

Model Opportunities

If you are one of those students who scored high in visual-spatial intelligence and believe you have an even higher predisposition for spatial intelligence, then you have an endless amount of strategies to employ to capitalize on what you're learning. You probably already do this naturally to an extent, but in general, any opportunity you have to visualize and manipulate things in your mind and with your hands is powerful.

Take your thinking further and analyze in your mind what the impact of any changes might be to various processes. Seeing models, how they work, and taking the opportunity to tinker with them will not only be natural and fun, but extremely useful. Getting your hands on and manipulating physical objects is of high importance, so take the initiative to create those opportunities for yourself, especially if they're not being provided. Putting ideas in terms of forms and pictures on paper will help you comprehend better. It's good to move around as part of your learning process, so talk to your teacher about having an opportunity to do so when it's appropriate.

Rather than discuss generalities, let's take a more specific look at how to use this faculty within a few specific disciplines. In science for example, do as many hands-on experiments as possible. Ask to see demonstrations whenever you can. While a teacher can tell you about density, having an opportunity to place an egg and watch it sink in plain water, then float in salt water, will have a more powerful impact for your comprehension.

Quick science experiments like that exist for so many of the concepts you're responsible for learning, whether it's osmosis, diffusion, photosynthesis, inertia, energy, centripetal force, condensation, surface tension, etc. Creating a collage of plants and animals, or a concept map with pictures for the water cycle, or going outside and seeing those things in nature with your own eyes, while discussing them, will benefit you more than simply reading or hearing about it.

In history, try seeing, drawing, sculpting and painting old historical scenes, civilizations and people and go to museums as much as possible. Drawing a map with regard to a distance scale and then putting it up on a wall where you can see it regularly will be information that stays with you permanently. In Math, manipulate objects (toothpicks, coins, jelly beans, etc.) for numbers or envision numbers and variables as objects for equations. Pick up every-day objects and measure them in various units. Also, for fun, play as many people in chess or Pictionary as you can. You might even surprise yourself how good you get!

Visual Intelligence

Have you ever heard a friend describe someone, someplace or something with such incredible detail that you can almost see it? It might have been a complete stranger they only met briefly, yet they give such a detailed description of that person from their hair type, color and length to their skin tone, shape of their nose, color of their eyes and dimples. They may include any distinguishing marks like a birthmark, tattoo or scar and go on about their height, body type, and weight estimate before mentioning the way they dress and walk. Yet, some other people can't even describe their best friend or own spouse with half that amount of detail!

Perhaps you know someone who took a vacation and described to you the surroundings of the place they visited with such vivid characteristics that you almost felt like you took a temporary vacation yourself to that same place. Maybe they were giving you directions as you were driving with such incredible particulars that you swore they were looking through a mini Go Pro camera strapped to your head and saw everything you did as you were driving. They may say, "When you get off at exit 26 for Storrow drive, you'll see the Fleet center on your left, but you'll need to navigate through current construction and the road will twist slightly to the right where you'll see the old brick state house on your left, but don't miss the first stop sign on the right after the state house because some tree branches are hanging in front of it." The old saying, "A picture is worth a thousand words" couldn't be truer if you or a friend fit the description of this kind of person because it defines one who has an extremely high level of Visual Intelligence.

Generally speaking, learners with a high faculty in this area think in pictures rather than words. They can visualize the world accurately and recreate aspects of what they experienced visually. They're good at fine details, especially with images, faces and places.

In general, I've found that most classrooms are better suited to meet the needs of a student who is a visual learner more than a spatial learner, not that the two are mutually exclusive. Most classrooms aren't short on visuals. In most classrooms, you can easily find posters, graphic organizers, concept maps and picture illustrations within the books, presentations or website you're studying. However, if you are a visual learner, it's your responsibility to take these strategies further and make sure the visual input you're receiving is a regular, relevant part of your daily learning process.

For example, you should **take advantage of any opportunity to draw**. It's a powerful technique to redraw a picture or concept map your teacher put on the whiteboard or smartboard. If time is short, ask if you can take a picture with your phone because for you, that picture is a quick gateway toward deep comprehension. Remember that drawing will have a more powerful impact on you because you're actively participating in the creation process.

On your own time, watch additional learning videos. In today's YouTube era, you can find an instructional video on literally anything you want to learn or understand. I'm huge fans of both Bozeman Science and Khan Academy myself. In addition, if you have access, VR devices play right into the hands of the visual learner, as well as the interpersonal and kinesthetic one.

If you're dealing with a lot of reading or text, you must use your highlighter! Try annotating in the margins in terms of symbols or initials while you're reading. It will help you access information in your mind more easily later on.

In addition, if you ever have to "memorize" words, **create different colored flashcards**! While I'm not the biggest fan of the word memorization, it will sometimes be a reality as a starting point to empower you to comprehend more complex ideas. Just remember that you should always be pushing yourself up Bloom's Taxonomy to apply, synthesize and analyze information. So, if you do have to memorize, such as Latin root prefixes and suffixes, which is often a reality for students in the sciences, then colored flash cards can help you categorize and remember them more easily. After you've memorized your flash cards, which will foster visual senses, then take the opportunity to apply those words by seeing how they are used, which will push you further up Bloom's Taxonomy through application. That task can easily be accomplished simply by typing the Latin root word into a search engine like Google and seeing the first word that pops up.

The last piece of that particular process would be drawing a quick sketch of the person, place or thing that you read about when you searched for the word, which taps back into your visual-spatial intelligence. After that, you'll find that you can't forget the Latin root word or its meaning even if you tried!

Phil And The Science Fair

I once had a student (let's call him Phil) at South Boston high school who had been in special education classes all of his academic life. Phil was an incredible human being, extremely respectful, mature and courageous, but struggled with dyslexia and needed more time than others to process information. Phil, along with a bunch of other students in special education, ended up in my mainstream chemistry class as part of our "inclusion" classroom, one that placed these students in the same classroom as mainstream students to ensure everyone is receiving the same level of academic rigor. It was a large class, and we had well over 50 students in it. Two teachers led the class – the regular teacher (me) handled the mainstream class and the special education teacher, who would work on "scaffolding" (breaking down) the material, met the needs of the special education students.

At the time the inclusion class started, we were already in the middle of the year and were working on Science Fair Projects in our mainstream class, which was a huge undertaking. Students were responsible for developing their own personal experiment, with an extensive log book detailing the process, and an in-depth research paper and summarizing display board. They employed the scientific method by creating their own testable question and experimental design, conducting a controlled experiment, analyzing their data, proving or disproving their hypothesis, and so on.

Most students in special education were not accustomed to doing project-based work of that magnitude. At first, Phil was a bit overwhelmed at the work he was responsible for on this project. However, I noticed something he was doing naturally, all the time, which was his ace in the hole. Phil loved to doodle. Sketching incredible cartoons, action heroes and cars in the margins of his notes and papers came naturally to him and he was great at it. He had an incredible, rich, natural faculty for visual-spatial intelligence right at his fingertips.

Speaking of which, Phil had also broken his hand at the time, so we decided to tap into both of these personal experiences for his project. Phil decided to do an experiment on the effect of various rehabilitation strategies on the physical improvement and mobility of his hand. Phil started by filling his log book with all these incredible brainstorming ideas. He then figured out his independent variable that he was going to manipulate and dependent variable he was going to study as a result of those brainstorming sketches so he had his testable question. Phil found several subjects to test, which included himself.

His log book was a piece of art! It had all these incredible sketches comparing his hand to other subjects. The illustrations he drew showed how and why different rehabilitation strategies were beneficial. Phil's research paper also contained rich visual illustrations of where he had broken his own metacarpal bone, concept maps of the different rehabilitative strategies, and creative graphical comparisons of other bone breaks similar in nature. Lastly, his display board was the most artistic and informative visual representation of the collected data that I had ever seen.

Above all else, Phil had fun. Watching him become more and more motivated with every passing minute he invested into that project proved he had found his well of motivation because Phil discovered himself through the process. He had tapped into his innate faculties and flourished as a result. Phil, of course, was excited to enter his project with all the other projects at our school's fair.

South Boston's annual Science Fair had become a huge event after I starting teaching there. Every single student taking science participated in the fair, and since science is a required course, that meant every student in the school competed, which tallied well over 400 students. Over 20 judges from various universities and corporations volunteered to come every year to objectively score different student projects by scrutinizing the work they did on their research paper, log book and display boards. In addition, the students were required to give an oral explanation to carefully explain to the judges how and what they did. Occasionally, the annual Science Fair at South Boston got so big that Thomas Menino, the mayor of Boston, and Deval Patrick, the Governor of Boston, attended the event, along with several members of the press. So, what was the outcome?

Phil took third place at our school wide Science Fair, which included everyone in the school, not just students in special education. To give you an idea of the level of competition he was up against, the student who won our school wide science fair ended up going on to compete in the State Science Fair at MIT and took third place there, which won her a $40,000 scholarship to Regis College.

Phil's example of success is one of many that proves we are all smart. By learning how you are smart, you not only will tap into an invaluable resource to help you learn, but you will also find inspiration and fun because the work will come naturally. Phil went on to serve our country as a US marine with several tours to Iraq. He has a beautiful family with two children and a very successful career. He still keeps in touch once in a while on Facebook and remembers everything he did and learned on that particular project to this day. To say I'm proud of him is an understatement.

MR. PFAFF'S TAKEAWAYS

- Concept map big ideas and draw pictures to represent information.

- Use symbols while taking notes and a highlighter when reading text.

- Color code information with different colored pencils, highlighters or notecards, especially when preparing for assessments.

- Watch teaching videos.

CHAPTER 8 Linguistic Intelligence

"The limits of my language are the limits of my world."

– Ludwig Wittgenstein, philosopher

Are you or someone you know one of those readers who can hear words, sentences and phrases in your mind as they're being read? Perhaps you might even be mumbling the words under your breath as you read in order to process information more efficiently. Do you tend to write notes (I'm a sticky note fanatic) for a "to do" list? When you recall a memory, are you more apt to remember the event linguistically?

In other words, do you more easily recall not only what a person said, but how they said it, as opposed to the environment in which the event took place or how you were feeling at the time? Or with a song, do you hear and recall the language more easily than the music itself? Do you often write to communicate ideas or convey emotions through language rather than through physicality or introspection? Can you speak more than one language and do you have the ability to quickly pick up speech patterns, inflections and words in additional languages? Perhaps you're good at quickly assimilating into another person's accent or dialect? If the answer is yes, then you are a very strong linguistic/auditory learner and you probably scored relatively high in this particular area.

In today's day and age, besides having strong intrapersonal intelligence, I find this particular gateway toward comprehension to be the most efficient, especially in terms of your time. If you are able to listen to information, ideas, messages, etc. and process it efficiently in real time, then you are in the driver's seat in terms of utilizing the amount of learning time you have in your day. To state the obvious, **people who are strong in this particular area learn well by speaking and listening to language.** They process and recall what they hear when teachers speak in class, during lectures, and what they heard in a video or on TV more quickly. Because of the nature of this particular input channel, you could pretty much do it anywhere.

Unlike interpersonal learning where you need another person, kinesthetic where you need to move and work with tangibles, or visual-spatial where you need to be seeing visual conception in some manner, all you need with linguistic is your ears and mouth, which you tend to carry with you wherever you go.

Audio Input

I remember working with a tutor my freshman year at Penn State University who was getting ready to apply to medical school. He was impressive to say the least – an All-American wrestler for Penn State University who had maintained a 4.0 G.P.A.

for the past two years. Since he was a pre-med student in his senior year, he tutored younger students taking biology to brush up on his own content knowledge. Even more important than the content knowledge I picked up from him was his work habits, especially with time management. He taught me to use my ears for learning more frequently, especially during "down times."

For example, he asked, "How much time do you spend walking around campus between classes on a daily basis?" I replied, "I don't know, probably well over an hour." In reality, at a huge university like Penn State with 40,000 people on campus, it was probably closer to 90 minutes every day, just walking. He then recommended using that time for learning by audio taping professors during class lectures, or reading my notes into a tape recorder and listening to them while I walked. And nowadays, nearly everything comes in an audiobook format.

His suggestion sounded a bit extreme to me at first, but I was so busy adapting to both college level academics and college athletics – we were running nearly 100 miles a week during the cross-country season – that I took his advice. Time was precious!

The results I had simply by putting on a pair of headphones when I walked around campus made a huge, immediate impact. The amount of information that I was able to learn, reinforce and remember was astounding. I actually surprised myself. That daily practice ended up not only improving my class performance, but cutting down on the study time I had to do at night to prepare for major exams. Overall, it saved time, reduced stress, and made me happier.

When I reflect on that technique, I realize it was tapping into other areas as well. As with most athletes, I'm also a very kinesthetic person. The fact that I was moving my body simply by walking while listening to this information just made it easier for me to process, as opposed to listening while I was laying down. In addition, everyone has different energy levels and they change throughout the day. Mine were much higher in the morning, so when I listened to this information as I walked to my first 8:00am class, it sank in much more easily than if I tried to take in that same information at 8:00pm at night after a full day of classes and workouts.

Today, nearly everyone carries a cell phone in their pocket. Your ability to listen to audio books, podcasts, YouTube videos, class lectures (if your teacher allows you to tape), etc. are at your fingertips almost all the time. When you start to analyze your day with this in mind, you'd be shocked at all the opportunities you have while you're walking, sitting outside eating lunch, on the bus, driving (if you're old enough), exercising or when you're just relaxing at home.

Help With Mundane Tasks

Have you ever tried doing a mundane physical task like cleaning, landscaping or house painting with headphones on? You'd be amazed how quickly the task gets completed and how much fun you had doing it! Linguistic intelligence does not have to be your highest faculty for you to tap into some of these powerful learning techniques either, you just have to take action by incorporating the techniques. In fact, I argue that you can't afford not to tap into this specific habit.

Listening to information is far from the only way to use your intelligence in this particular area though. It's just one of the more time-efficient ones since you can multi-task. **Just make sure you practice sound judgment by not using headphones during a task that requires your undivided attention,** such as juggling knives.

Additional Tools

Additional techniques useful for the linguistic learner would be grasping ideas in terms of a verbal debate or journaling of some kind. Have fun with jokes, puns and literary interpretation, as well. For example, creating your own story, in an effort to comprehend a historical event, would work extremely well, especially when you say it out loud, as you should with any written technique. Mock trials, acting, teaching others and interviews are additional tools you can utilize while working cooperatively with others. My father, who has a great sense of humor, always says if you want to remember a good joke, you have to tell it at least once. He's right, especially if you're a linguistic learner.

Mnemonic Devices

Have you ever been tasked with having to remember and recall a lot of content on your own? We all have! Think about those content-driven courses such as history and science. If you're a linguistic learner, mnemonic devices, particularly name mnemonics, are one of the most useful techniques you can use to remember information. A mnemonic is a sentence, phrase, word or even model to help you remember separate objects, ideas and elements that make up a group. Often, the fun thing about a mnemonic device is that the sillier it is, the easier it is to remember and use to recall more complex content. I'm sure you've already heard some commonly used mnemonics like, "Please Excuse My Dear Aunt Sally" to remind you of the order of operations in math (parentheses, exponents, multiplication, division, addition, subtraction) or Roy G. Biv (red, orange, yellow, green, blue, indigo and violet) to remember color spectrums in science.

Chances are, if it's a universal piece of content knowledge you're required to learn in any given discipline, a mnemonic device has already been established. So why reinvent the wheel? If it's already laid out for you and you have a faculty for linguistic intelligence, use it.

I often tutor students in biology and chemistry at different schools all over the country. When learning about oxidation reduction reactions, I've found all chemistry teachers make their students memorize the mnemonic OIL RIG (oxidation is loss, reduction is gain) to get them to remember which elements and molecules are losing or gaining electrons. Within a second, chemistry students are always able to quickly recall what's happening with electrons during reactions using that particular mnemonic. However, at the same time, I've personally found that it's also extremely fun for students to create their own mnemonic if one doesn't exist, especially if they're getting bored with the material. In biology, I was taught the mnemonic "Place My Aunt to Congo" to recall the order of the phases of Mitosis (Prophase, Metaphase, Anaphase, Telophase, Cytokinesis), but it usually doesn't work well for students, so I have them invent their own, which they've taken some liberties with to say the least. Even when I see them two or three years later as seniors in my physiology course, they still remember the mnemonics they invented as freshmen.

Mnemonic devices aren't just in name form though, they can be music, expression, rhyme, image and connection as well. Have you ever tried remembering the lyrics to a song without the music in your head? It's hard. Suddenly, if you can recall the melody, beat and rhythm of the song, the lyrics rush back into your brain in an instant. Advertisers are especially aware of this fact and actually capitalize on it during radio and TV spots so consumers have it in their head, making them more apt to buy the product.

Ever hear the phrase, "Let's get ready to rumble!" before a big boxing match? If you have, chances are extremely high that you're remembering the rhythm and inflection in which it's said, as well – probably more than the words themselves. Michael Buffer, who came up with it, was so aware of the memory power of catchphrases that he decided to trademark it. He now gets paid $5 million every time he says it. Talk about capitalizing on linguistics!

From coordinating conjunctions in English to recalling gas laws in chemistry, expression mnemonics are also extremely useful. Expression mnemonics remind you of an underlying principle even though each letter doesn't correspond with a word. An example would be, "To remember good old Hank, remember the bubbles in the shaken Coke you drank," to recall Henry's Law which states the solubility of a gas increases with pressure.

Personally, if I'm trying to remember which months of the year have 28 days, I still recite to myself the lines I learned in second grade, "30 days hath September, April, June, and November. All the rest have 31, except for February which has 28." On a larger scale, I've seen students write their own rap songs with catchy, informative lyrics that would blow your mind, not to mention help you ace an exam. Those examples would be that of a rhyme mnemonic, another valuable type you can utilize.

A model, such as the one used to illustrate Bloom's Taxonomy, would be in the mnemonic category as well, but that example might resonate more with your visual spatial faculty. The same applies to image mnemonics which accomplish the same goal with pictures in a certain arrangement to help you recall.

Lastly a connection mnemonic is a phenomenal tool that students can use to transfer new information over to long term memory by connecting something new they heard to something they already knew. I mentioned previously an example of this when I described a greenstick fracture. This one technique is a very powerful way to remember new material permanently.

Benefits Of Linguistic Intelligence

One of the greatest benefits of being strong in this particular intelligence, in my opinion, is the ability to comprehend and speak foreign languages. If you were raised in a bilingual or trilingual home, you already have an advantage. If you weren't, I encourage you to commit yourself to learning another language using your own self-learned tool box, even if you scored low on linguistic intelligence. Nelson Mandela is quoted saying, "If you talk to a man in a language he understands, that goes to his head. If you talk to him in his language, that goes to his heart." Nothing can be truer.

Very often, it's extremely difficult to truly understand the significance of culture, art, relationships and politics unless you're hearing it expressed in the native language. To speak another language effectively is to know another culture intimately. Just because you're raised in a bilingual home, though, doesn't mean speaking a second language will be easy or that you're high in linguistic intelligence. It's up to you to self-discover your own strengths and use those strengths to your learning advantage.

I grew up with a friend whose parents only spoke Italian around the house and spoke very limited English. They had four kids. The two older siblings spoke Italian fluently and the two younger ones didn't. So, it doesn't come naturally for everyone, but it might to you. Find your own unique gateway to the inside of that looking glass by knowing yourself, such as the person in my next example, Timothy Doner.

Tim Doner is such a great example when it comes to the power of a linguistic learner. If you haven't heard of him, just type his name into YouTube, you can't miss him. He's a teenage phenomenon who has gotten national attention due to the fact that he "speaks" 23 languages, not to mention they were self-taught. If you watch his interviews and explanations on how he did it though, it makes perfect sense. Since Tim was good at making sounds and doing various accents and dialects as a child, he became an actor doing various radio spots, voice over work and TV ads. His intrapersonal knowledge about his linguistic intelligence was revealed to him early in life, which empowered him to accomplish these other impressive feats with language in his teenage years.

Even more astounding than his ability to speak so many languages is the intrapersonal knowledge he exemplifies in his interviews, which got him to the point where he is today. Tim knew himself well enough to know where his passions were. To him, experimenting with various languages was as fun of a pastime as a kinesthetic learner would have shooting foul shots on a basketball court.

Tim Doner has enough self-knowledge to garner the courage to test out his language skills by walking around the diverse sub-cultures in various communities of New York City to have conversations with, and learn from, native speakers.

He has enough self-knowledge to clearly state that even with his unique strength, it took a lot of grinding, testing and trial and error to get to where he is. He also has enough self-knowledge and humility to repeatedly tell the press he can't actually speak 23 languages fluently, even though they ignore it in efforts to sensationalize his story and sell news. Tim is a true example of a student of life who "knows thyself." If you can't relate to Tim Doner's story, try looking at someone who likes to leverage their linguistic/auditory intelligence into writing instead.

Lisa, Alice and *Hamilton*

I took an acting class in Boston years ago with a good friend named Lisa. She was talented in so many ways, but one of her strengths that always stood out was her ability to translate her imagination, heart and passion into written language. She'd often go to write at a Starbucks before or after we'd rehearse together for a scene we were doing in class. Although she had never been an author before, Lisa had enough intrapersonal intelligence to know her own motivations and necessary daily habits to take on the demanding endeavor of writing a novel.

Her daily routines which made use of these particular strengths became her habits of work and mind and she eventually finished her novel and self-published the book in 2007. She started by selling copies of the book out of the trunk of her car, until finally, a major publisher discovered her book and acquired it.

Lisa's book eventually landed on the *New York Times* best seller list for 59 weeks. It's been translated into 36 languages, is sold in over 30 countries, and has over 2.6 million copies in print. After its release, one of the largest talent agencies in Los Angeles bought the rights to the book to make a movie out of it. Known as the film, *Still Alice*, Julianne Moore won the best actress Oscar award for playing its lead role. Lisa has since written three more novels, which are all *New York Times* best sellers. It all started with an unknown author who knew herself well enough to start utilizing her linguistic intelligence. So, if you have a strong faculty in this area and have the intrapersonal intelligence required to fully commit yourself to a task, then a career as an author might be right for you.

Another great example of a person who can leverage this innate linguistic ability is Lin-Manuel Miranda, the song writer and lyricist behind the brilliance of the Broadway play, *Hamilton*. To say Lin-Manuel has strong linguistic intelligence is an understatement. However, it took him two years of writing and walking while listening to a loop of piano music, just to get the first two songs completed!

Hamilton would not be the masterpiece it is if Lin Manuel didn't also have extreme intrapersonal knowledge, which empowered him to capitalize on his linguistic strengths and stay focused on his path. It's the same reason that is at the heart of what lead any rap artist to fame. Jay Z, Ice Cube, Biggie Smalls, Tupac and Eminem are just a few of the amazing artists with a powerful ability to leverage language to capture truth, a truth that only they can tell. If you're not a believer, I encourage you to watch how confident, articulate, and passionate any one of these gentlemen are in an interview. I'm still blown away at the insightful, historically accurate, passionate interviews Ice Cube gave throughout his career, but especially during the controversial release of NWA's "F#ck tha Police" back in the late 80s."

You don't have to be a celebrity, however, to find a great career which puts the strengths of the linguistic learner to use. Lawyers, writers, radio/TV announcers, journalists, curators, speech pathologists, food critics, advertising and copywriters are just a few who flourish in everyday society.

Are you one of those people who has an opinion on everything? My wife is (by the way if you're reading this, dear, please don't jump to conclusions until I've made my point). She always seems to capture the perfect words to describe what she likes or doesn't like about everything, whether it is a movie, song, performer or food. Plus, she can do it in both English and Spanish, as she speaks both languages perfectly. So, if you have the inclination to say what you like or dislike about things, a career as a critic will capitalize on your linguistic faculty.

The Great Persuader

I grew up with two good childhood friends who both have a gift for persuasion. One of them always seemed to be able to convince us to do things, whether it was something simple like seeing a movie he wanted to see or something more taxing like riding our dirt bikes all the way to the George Washington Bridge from Maywood, New Jersey. The other friend always seemed to get us to adopt his opinion using persuasive language. It could be something simple like why I should dislike a muffin from a certain bakery for having too many blueberries to larger things like why I should use my professional teaching experience to write this book.

The power of persuasive language happens to be the basis of advertising. Therefore, it doesn't surprise me that my friend Tom just opened up his own advertising company, Morris Media Group, and my other friend Al has traveled the world for major retail companies and teaches marketing courses at four different major universities in New York. So, if you have a strong faculty in this area and happen to be that friend who can talk your other friends into anything, a career in advertising or sales might be perfect for you.

Public Speaking

Not everyone enjoys public speaking. In fact, it's been noted and generally accepted in psychology circles that most people fear public speaking more than death itself! When I was teaching public speaking as an adjunct professor at Suffolk University, I experienced this fact first hand. I even had a student who developed skin rashes due to the anxiety she felt about giving a speech to our small class of 15 students!

In my opinion, public speaking is a required skill you'll need, whether you're presenting in class, on a job interview, or talking to your teammates before a big game. It can be mastered with continual practice even if you aren't high on the linguistic scale. That being said, a few select other people actually relish in public speaking. Those particular types can put together words to inform and entertain others even in the most unforeseeable circumstances. If you're one of those rare people, then consider putting your linguistic competency to work as a host, announcer, party emcee or auctioneer. Who knows, maybe you'll even copyright the next great catch phrase like Michael Buffer.

MR. PFAFF'S TAKEAWAYS

- Record class lectures and read information into a recording device on a regular basis.

- Use headphones to listen to information throughout your busy day.

- Use mnemonic devices, verbal debates, songs and rhymes to process and remember.

CHAPTER 9 Habits of Work and Mind

"We are what we repeatedly do. Excellence, then, is not an act, but a habit."

> *– Will Durant, writer and philosopher*

Let's take a pragmatic look at ourselves and ask, "What are your current habits as a student?"

More specifically, are you aware of both good and poor habitual behaviors inside and outside the classroom that you do or do not do, either consciously or unconsciously? Chances are you haven't thought about that question to such an extent, but finding your answer to that question is a necessity not only as a student, but in life.

In this chapter, I'll be giving you some overarching philosophies that will help guide your actions as a whole, but also, very specific day-to-day tasks you should be doing in order to find great success as a learner in life. In general, you should already know by now that it's your responsibility to strengthen your intrapersonal intelligence – what your personal motivations and strengths are and various learning strategies you can tap into to capitalize on them. Having that personal knowledge will help guide you to more specific day-to-day steps. For example, if you're more of an interpersonal learner, initiating dialog with your teacher, finding a peer with whom you can discuss content (in person, Skype, FaceTime, etc.) for each class and regularly talking with others is a habit you should engage in daily.

On the other hand, if you're more visual/spatial, then watching videos, creating concept maps, models and using pictures and symbols to take notes should be a daily practice. If you're more kinesthetic, you need to find a way to move your body, and get a tactile, hands-on experience to understand more efficiently, etc.

The Law Of Attraction

Let's talk in general terms before we get to the very specific, easy, daily rituals you can use. While the specific details are easy, the general habits of work and mind take a lot more analysis and effort. I'm sure you've heard of the law of attraction before. In simple terms, this law of the universe states that what you focus on the most in your mind, whether it be positive or negative, is what you will attract in your life. The underlying reason is because, on a conscious and subconscious level, you make choices (don't forget that doing nothing is still a choice) and therefore take actions that brings you closer to what you're focusing on and this eventually will manifest itself into reality.

It's powerful, it's real and you can use these laws to guide you toward anything you truly desire. The cool thing about this phenomenon is that through practice, we can learn to guide our own thoughts, and subsequently, the feelings associated with those thoughts. How do we monitor our own thoughts? We're only limited by our own imagination and effort.

Just like a child who plays with figurines in an imaginary moment and answers mom in real time, and then goes back to the imaginary world, you can do the same thing. Through imaginary focus, you can bring your thoughts and subsequent feelings to another place, simply by using the power of your mind. That mind power has always been at work for you whether you realize it or not. In addition, you've always had the power to change your thought patterns and the associated feelings that come with them, whenever you want. You just have to be conscious of that mind power, which is at your disposal at all times.

For example, say you're having a good time at lunch, hanging out with a good friend when she brings up a substitute teacher she heard she's going to have in her next class. Unbeknownst to her, you had that same substitute teacher last week and didn't like her at all because the sub kicked you out of class for talking too much! Within an instant, your thoughts go back to the embarrassing, negative experience you had with that sub last week and you tell your friend about it. As you're retelling the story, your voice gets louder and you find yourself getting angrier and angrier. Suddenly, you're not feeling so great anymore. Emotionally, you were in a completely different place just minutes ago, laughing with your friend until you relived in your mind that negative experience. Maybe retelling that story during lunch had such a negative impact on you that you were hesitant to speak up and volunteer in your next class after lunch. As a result, you weren't as engaged in the material that day and didn't learn to the best of your ability, which effected your quiz score at the end of the week, etc.

That downward cycle is an example of something that was all sparked by a thought in your mind. On the other hand, take a moment right now to focus on an accomplishment you've had in your life that you're proud of, or an image of your most beloved place on earth, or simply your favorite dessert. Whatever you choose, really focus on it. If you focus long enough, you might find you're a bit more relaxed, maybe even smiling without knowing it. Whatever unforeseen incident happens to you in the next few minutes, chances are you'll approach it with more optimism, strength and focus then the previous example.

Neither one of those incidents happened in the present. Where you chose to put your focus and imagination is what made the difference. What's even more exciting is that you can get better at this technique with practice, just like many other things.

The question is, though, how accurately do you evaluate reality? In other words, based on past experiences, do you perceive new tasks that might seem challenging from a place of fear or anxiety?

Are your present-day reactions to demanding tasks based on an old, out-of-date script you keep following on a conscious or subconscious level? Is that script even accurate? More importantly, does your script serve you for the better? If you're unsure, once again, you need to self-analyze because your mind might be engaging in a habit you're unaware of.

True Grit

Angela Lee Duckworth is a psychologist, science author, and former middle school math teacher who came up with some intriguing research that can help find the answers to those questions. She collected data on a variety of people, young and old, in various professions, to see what ultimately determined how successful they were. The data in her massive study concluded that the biggest impact on success wasn't IQ, social intelligence, or even good health. It was grit.

Grit can be described as the passion, perseverance and stamina to continue trying a task, especially when it's challenging. After the first time that I watched Angela's discussion on *Ted Talks*, I looked up at a quote that I've had on every desk wall since college.

"Nothing in this world can take the place of persistence. Talent will not; nothing is more common than unsuccessful men with talent. Genius will not; unrewarded genius is almost a proverb.

Education will not; the world is full of educated derelicts. Persistence and determination alone are omnipotent." – Calvin Coolidge

While I don't agree with the way Mr. Coolidge used the word "education" (I wish he used "schooling" instead), I do believe those words speak an inevitable truth. Every good teacher ultimately knows this truth – that grit will pay off. It's the same reason why Dweck says a student with a growth mindset will flourish over a student with a fixed one.

So how do we develop a grit-growth mindset?

Know thyself through intrapersonal intelligence. If you know what kind of learner you happen to be, say for example, a musical one, then creating a rap song that describes the organelle functions in a cell is going to be of more interest and impact than reading about it or looking at a picture. The time you put into that task will pay off because you will have a deeper understanding of how your own personal brain processes information. That being said, you will need to practice the techniques, whether it be a general mind approach, like redirecting negative thinking, or a more specific action task such as speaking and listening to a tape recorder to process and recall content specific information.

In addition, **find purpose in what you're doing by facing challenging tasks from a broader**

perspective. A narrow perspective would be one in which a student says I don't see the point in having to learn the trigonometric functions. A broader one would be to remind yourself that if you can find a way to master trigonometric function using your own personal innate faculties, then you can accomplish anything your math teacher, or any other teacher, will throw at you. Now there's an overarching reason to see that specific task through!

You can also develop grit by having hope. Even if a circumstance or challenge seems hopeless, remember that hope can be borrowed, learned and taught. If you're feeling hopeless, find someone who has hope, who speaks, believes and lives it. Call me biased, but teachers are a pretty good place to start if you're looking to borrow some inspiration.

On the contrary, be careful about spending too much time around negative people. Chronically negative people seldom spread a sense of grit. In fact, if you allow them, they can sabotage your own senses of passion and perseverance. Instead, surround yourself with gritty people. To this day, I know I could bank on any teammate I ran with at Penn State University to help me through a problem and to set an example on how to thrive because of the pure grit you find in most distance runners, especially those who had the privilege to run under the tutelage of head coach Harry R. Groves.

Fast And Slow Thinking

A similar but even more analytical way to look at the general habits of your mind concerning day-to-day problems and challenges is what psychology professor and Nobel prize winner Daniel Kahneman has classified as System 1 and System 2 thinking.

To simplify his classification ever further, System 1 is "fast" thinking while System 2 is "slow" thinking. In other words, fast thinking is that intuitive, in the moment kind of thinking one does, which is largely based on prior knowledge. People tend to revert to this kind of thinking more often because it's faster and easier, but people also tend to make more mistakes with System 1 fast thinking. If too many opportunities to succeed are lost due to System 1 thinking, it's easier to lose that sense of self-worth when it comes to problem solving. The result can very often be lost momentum and motivation to sustain effort on difficult tasks.

System 2, or slow thinking, is more analytical and slower. It's harder because that kind of decision-making weighs in more factors that can improve the accuracy of your conclusion, so it takes more time. System 2 thinking requires an objective formulaic approach, so employing self-discipline and patience are imperative. These results, however, in seizing more opportunities to succeed, and this can improve your sense of self-worth when facing challenges and problems and reinforce the motivation to really take the extra time to think.

So how do you know if you're operating out of System 1 or System 2? First off, just being aware of these two levels of thinking can prompt you to become more analytical during daily problem solving. Before you deliver an answer to any kind of question, my suggestion is to also simply ask yourself, "Is there more to consider?"

In addition, self-centering techniques such as deep breathing, progressive relaxation and checking in with yourself can help get yourself into a more productive state of mind to operate in System 2 more often. You can even download apps such as "Stop, Breath and Repeat" which prompts the user to check in with themselves and makes "mindfulness" recommendations, based on the answers the user gives to the application prompts. These help center your mind, body and spirit.

Many options to center yourself exist, but you have to take that initiative. Frequent check-ins will give you more of the focus and fortitude to apply analytical thinking to problem solving.

Taking Initiative

Now that we've discussed the general habits of work and mind, let's take a look at some simple, easy-to-manage strategies that you should be doing on a regular basis in all classrooms. One of the first habits of work and mind you should remember is to be proactive, not reactive. In other words, always take initiative. While you should never shy away from asking any question to your teacher, teachers do love proactive students who have taken steps to try to answer a question or solve a problem on their own first rather than simply asking for an answer without putting forth any thought or effort.

An example could be looking up the meaning of a word and then asking for further explanation from your teacher rather than just asking what a word means. Never ask a teacher to do something that you can easily do yourself. Trying to find, or asking if you can look for, the material or equipment you need when doing a class lab or project is much more self-empowering than asking your teacher to get it for you.

Also, it could be something more involved such as attempting to comprehend a concept or problem you've been covering in class with a concerted, personal effort. Coming up with your own questions and areas of confusion, based on the work you put in, which you ask your teacher to clarify, is a habit you want to be in. Try to avoid simply asking the teacher to re-explain the whole concept without having identified your own personal areas of confusion.

Proactive students are the type of students who always know what is coming up in class by reviewing material they're covering ahead of time, even if nothing tangible needs to be turned into the teacher for a grade. Reactive students are the type of students who go into a panic because they just found out they have a quiz tomorrow, or worse – today – that they're unprepared for.

While in class, "owning" what you don't know by seeking "discomfort" is one of the best habits you can be in. In other words, raise your hand if you're confused! Students actually learn the most when they are struggling to understand a concept, not when the comprehension comes easy and is "comfortable." Being the first one to raise your hand in class will take some guts, but it is worth it.

Don't worry about what your peers think when you ask questions in class because chances are they have the same question you do, but haven't worked up the courage to ask. The secret is to put yourself in that position early and often. Do not wait.

If you fall into the poor habit of not raising your hand when you don't understand something in class, not only will it negatively impact your ability to understand that one problem or concept in the moment, but it will disengage you from the material over a longer period of time. Break the ice and try it. When you do this, you also change the culture and climate of the classroom because it encourages your peers to ask more questions as well, which has a tremendously powerful learning impact on the whole group!

In addition, have a regular routine which checks in with yourself and asks if you have given your best effort. Doing this will allow you to better distinguish your own good effort from a bad one and will condition you to sustain a real, focused effort over a longer period of time. Small day-to-day habits that take almost no effort can make a large difference in your overall success.

It might seem "old-school," but in western cultures it's best to introduce yourself to your teacher on the first day of class with a firm handshake and eye contact. That first impression advice goes for all professional work settings, not just the classroom. If you have the choice of seat selection, always choose to sit in front of the class. Numerous studies have been conducted on seat selection and data supports that students who sit in front tend to do better than those who sit toward the back. Sitting toward the front also has an impact on student-teacher rapport which could tap into your motivation, effort and concentration while in class.

Do not miss any homework assignments, especially during your first month of class. We all know circumstances can pop up occasionally, which can lead to a missed homework assignment, but if that happens within the first month of school, you might pay a bigger price than if you missed that same homework assignment toward the end of a grading period because of the perception it creates.

Good reputations can be built quickly in class, especially through conscientious homework delivery. If you establish a studious reputation early on, it will be easier to ask for extensions or exceptions later on during the grading period. If you miss a few submissions early on, a teacher may be less willing to make exceptions on your behalf. I don't advise missing any homework assignments, but if you have to, do it in the last half of the grading period, or better yet, the last half of the year.

Remember that trial and error are the real-life processes behind every meaningful learning process. You'll need to be open to continual adaptation as you find your rhythm with each new teacher, strategy and technique you have. In fact, many people's definition of success itself is simply, "the ability to adapt."

Be careful about sitting close to a friend who might distract you. To state the obvious, don't over socialize on things unrelated to the content you're discussing during class time. Too many times, I've seen students who lose concentration due to a friend talking to them about things unrelated to class. If prompting and redirection doesn't happen quickly enough, it can have a detrimental effect not only on your class performance, but on your motivation to truly engage the content as well.

At the same time, make an effort to gravitate towards friends who are good at discussing the class content with you. Even if you're not high on the interpersonal intelligence spectrum, you should find a peer to study with. And while we're on the topic of peer tutoring, try to detach yourself from an unhealthy dependency on paid tutors. A paid tutor outside of class is most useful when you're already employing the habits of intrapersonal intelligence and self-reliance.

While I didn't see the problem of paid tutors a lot when I was teaching in the Boston Public School system, I definitely see it working at an affluent private school in California. I'd say over 90% of the student population where I currently teach uses paid tutors outside of class. Unfortunately, I've occasionally seen an undesirable outcome from working with paid tutors because some students fall into a passive mode. They might be thinking, "Why should I learn this in class now, or use my planning period to do my best to comprehend it, when I can just learn it later from my tutor?" That kind of approach takes the onus off where it belongs – on you! It chips away at your ability to continually develop self-understanding, time management and your personal bag of learning tricks. Those aren't just skills you need in class, they are skills you will forever need for your own education in life.

If you're already using the self-analytical tools to utilize your strengths, and are seeing your teacher for extra help when you're confused, and are using your free time effectively, then a paid tutor might be useful. However, if you're waiting for your tutor to do your homework, which you haven't even attempted on your own yet, then you are wasting your time and money.

Good Classroom Behavior

Although this might seem like common knowledge, many students forget how to behave when they're in the classroom. If you get into a consistent habit of carrying yourself with a professional demeanor when you speak and act while you're in the classroom, then you'll be giving yourself an incredible advantage. If you are struggling with monitoring your own behavior or notice your teacher has to redirect you often during class, then you should get familiar with the term "code switching." Many different definitions exist for how people code switch, but I like to describe it simply by **remembering to use the appropriate way to express yourself given the people and environment you're interacting with**.

For example, you might talk to a friend in the locker room or on the athletic field much differently than you would talk to that same friend inside a classroom. If you don't, you're forgetting to code switch. Even the toughest, at risk, borderline youth I've taught would never speak to their grandma in a certain manner. Deep down, they know how to code switch. We all do. You just have to remember the classroom is no different. The old school saying, "there is a time and place for everything" captures this buzz word accurately.

Crude language or gestures, horsing around, excessive talking that's unrelated to what you're studying, putting your feet up on a desk, etc. are all inappropriate behaviors for the classroom. There is a time and place for you to talk and act that way, but it's not in the classroom. Not only will you be projecting a poor image of yourself to your peers and teacher, but you will be cutting your mind off from absorbing valuable knowledge you need to be successful in that class and in life.

> *"Chains of habit are too light to be felt until they are too heavy to be broken."*
> *- Warren Buffett, billionaire stock investor*

What are your daily habits of organization? Have you implemented a practical, effective system that personally works for your busy, complex life? If, on occasion, you have forgotten when homework, quizzes or tests are due, what you're covering in class, or even how you're going to effectively use a block of free time, then you should reevaluate your system. Jotting down important information on a random paper without transferring it to a master calendar can easily be forgotten.

Organizational Habits

Everyone has their own way of organizing, and while a calendar book is a good idea, chances are you don't have it on you at all times like you do a cell phone. Almost every student I have uses some sort of cell phone, very often an iPhone, which means they're carrying the power of a mini computer in their pocket wherever they go. While it's natural for them to text with friends, look up information on search engines, and find directions, not everyone is using the strong organizational tools these phones offer. If you're using an iPhone, both the calendar and reminder applications are extremely useful. If it's a different phone, you might have a different program, but it's the same organizational tools, at your fingertips. These programs give a quick, easy way to access what your day, week, or even month looks like at a glance. It quickly allows you to put in reminders for upcoming events with as much time notice as you want. The feature also allows you to add extra essential description notes that you can easily share with friends.

Most services even allow you to easily recover the calendar information if the phone is lost and can sync the information with other devices. You can set up a repeating reminder every day that prompts you of something you might forget, such as entering calendar information for a few minutes every day at 12:00pm.

If you learn how to use the system effectively, the system will start doing more of the organizational work for you. You'll get quicker and more detailed with how you enter calendar and reminder information, just as you are now probably very quick at finding your favorite emoji while texting (laughing face with tears of joy emoji seems to be most popular these days).

Daily details of what you're covering in class are important to enter even if you don't have an important test or assignment to hand in because it keeps the content you're covering in class relevant. While it might be hard to take out a cell phone during class when a teacher is making an announcement, you can easily transfer calendar information to your phone after class or during a free block.

The earlier you start the powerful habit of an effective organizational system, the better off you will be. It can be easy if you are very deliberate about being consistent when you start. Some students are forced to start organizing very early in life and the skills they possess by the time they're in high school can be profound. While the private school in the valley where I work might seem like the polar opposite of the public urban high school where I used to teach in Boston, many similarities still exits. The closer you look at real human beings, the more truths and traits of success can be seen no matter who you are or where you live. Universal themes of teenagers seeking acceptance, adapting to academic rigors, protecting their image, and discovering themselves exists everywhere, no matter where in the world you are. Everyone needs to learn their own system of organization which works for them.

For example, we have some extremely successful child actors who attend the high school where I teach. I've had some of these students in my class, and one of the traits that impresses me the most about them is their organizational habits. A lifetime of acting classes, auditions, rehearsals and performances has forced them to learn, through trial and error, how to manage their life. Receiving call sheets and negotiating times they have to be on set with class responsibilities has forced them not only to be extremely strong communicators and organizers, but to be extremely efficient with the time they do spend in class because it's less than the typical student. While these kinds of students are already very gifted and capable, the lifestyle they had to learn so early has a direct translation to the organizational habits they later need to be successful in the classroom.

On a similar note, I've had many students at South Boston who had to get up at 4:00am in order to take three different buses to school, only to work an after-school job and take care of their younger siblings. Those same students were forced to employ strong organizational habits long before high school in order to be successful at work, home and as a responsible older sibling. As a result, those early habits of work and mind they were forced to develop helped maintain academic success as well.

Taking early action toward finding an organizational system that works for you is an essential life skill, not just for school, so investing that time is worth it. It can be done, no matter where you are or what your situation is. The key is to start now, to be open to change if something better exists, to be very deliberate with using your system, and to always stay consistent with your approach.

Conditioning yourself to take a systematic, disciplined approach can take on many forms. For instance, you can use your school bell (or some other stimulus) at the beginning of each class to condition yourself to check in on your calendar details for the week for that one particular class. The ending bell can be your stimulus to input and review calendar details you're responsible for during the rest of the week for that same class. If you try that one simple approach for one full week, you might surprise yourself at how easily it becomes a habit.

Why is it important to be able to access the details of your day or week often and at a quick glance? For starters, it forces you to operate from that proactive, rather than reactive, state of mind. No event that you're responsible for will ever take you by surprise which is empowering in itself. An effective system of organization also keeps the content you're covering in class at the forefront of your mind, making it easier to comprehend for the next time you see it again. In addition, it reminds you of specific areas in which you may be confused, which allows you to take better advantage of the free time you have during the week to seek answers. After all, how can you seek an answer to a question you can't even remember? Lastly, it helps you develop more effective schemas for remembering information.

Schema

A schema is a simple technique to help you remember concepts and ideas through certain associations and groupings. For example, if I asked you to remember to go to the store next week and buy some duct tape, printing paper, spark plugs, tortilla chips, two wine glasses and some ball bearings, chances are high you might forget a few items, especially if you didn't write it down. However, if I asked you the same thing, but this time asked you to buy orange juice, eggs, bacon, potatoes, bread and coffee, chances are high you might remember all the items because you already have a schema for what breakfast is in your head.

A schema is an organizational process that happens in your mind. If you're not accessing the information you're covering in class on a regular basis, then you can't even begin to think about how you are grouping and associating that information in your brain. The result will be that the content will still seem new to you the next time you see it in class again.

Lastly, **remember that concentration is a skill that can be improved**. Even if you feel you're at a disadvantage in this area due to concentration issues such as ADHD, you can greatly improve your concentration with consistent, deliberate bouts of sustained effort.

The key to extending your concentration time is to first be aware of when your mind is drifting. Lots of different techniques exist to monitor when your mind drifts, which I'll address more in the chapter on anxiety. I personally tried a technique where I'd write a check mark at the top of my notes whenever my mind drifted during a study session. My goal was to decrease the amount of checks I saw at the top of my notes with each subsequent study session. I've known other people who take that self-conditioning concentration technique even further by wearing a rubber band around their wrist and snapping it against the inside of their wrist whenever their mind wondered.

Whatever calls your attention to a drifting mind and includes a method of continually minimizing drifting episodes is fine. I remember that during my freshman year at Penn State, it was very hard for me to sit down at my desk to study for even 30 minutes, especially after a long day of classes and workouts. However, I pushed myself every weekday and Sunday night (with Saturday night off of course) and by the end of my first semester, I was able to sit down at my desk for almost three hours, with only a few short, periodic breaks in-between.

MR. PFAFF'S TAKEAWAYS

- Hope and grit can be borrowed, learned and taught.

- Avoid negative thought patterns and negative people.

- Take initiative toward being self-reliant and don't be afraid to make mistakes.

- Ask yourself if there is more to consider when making decisions.

- Develop perseverance by sticking with challenging and boring tasks.

- Incorporate an organizational system that's easy to maintain and commit to it.

- Monitor when your concentration deviates in order to improve it.

- How you express yourself is governed by the environment you're in.

CHAPTER 10 Assessment

"Learners need endless feedback more than they need endless teaching."
                              – Grant Wiggins, author

Whether your school is calling your performance feedback portfolio, formative, summative, authentic, differentiated assessment, or any and all of the above, getting consistent feedback to understand your strengths and weaknesses is important. Even more informative, though, is discovering and clarifying your misconceptions, because that's the most critical part of your growth process as a learner.

We learn the most when we are making mistakes, asking questions, and clarifying confusion. According to Lloyd Alexander, an accomplished American author of over 40 books for young adults, "We learn more by looking for the answer to a question and not finding it than we do from learning the answer itself."

Unfortunately, in many school systems we get the direct and indirect message that making too many mistakes is a bad thing. When it comes to assessment, try to take a step back and look at the big picture. You might be asking yourself, "Why do I even need to be tested to begin with?" or "This teacher's tests are so hard," or simply, "I hate tests." While test scores, such as G.P.A, SAT, AP Exams,

MCAT, LSAT, do play a role in terms of college, grad school and certain job applications, it should not stop you from seeing them for what they are – learning tools.

Remember, your education and learning takes place everywhere and anywhere, not just in preparation for an exam within the school system. As long as you're continuing to learn about yourself, your motivations, strengths, passions, etc., then new doors will always open for you, very often at the exact time they're supposed to.

Sometimes test scores come across as a very impersonal statistic somewhere on the bell curve, so why should you give the score more importance than it deserves? Instead, take that impersonal feedback of a test score and personalize what you need from it to obtain the larger learning opportunity. In addition, if you do put the emphasis where it's supposed to be, which is using your education to personally learn the material to your best ability, then the grade you desire will often be there anyway.

I have a great friend who I went to high school with who wasn't motivated in high school. He was possibly even a bit depressed during those years. He wasn't taking college prep courses and didn't think much about his own learning process, motivations or passions. He reluctantly went to a community college after high school.

While he was there, however, a spark lit inside him. He discovered himself and a passion for the social condition. He started reading books about Gandhi's life and got very turned on to education. He started getting straight A's in his courses at the community college as a residual effect of that self-discovery, and he transferred to NYU where he continued to get straight A's. After graduating at the top of his class, he went on to get his MBA and now works and travels all over the world for a major retailer. In addition, he also gives back by teaching MBA courses at four different universities in New York.

School, or any facet it of it, is never the core reason for a lack of inspiration or personal success. It's education that has that power. Understand yourself, and the world will present itself to you. Billionaires, such as Richard Branson, Henry Ford, Carl Lindner, John D. Rockefeller and Kirk Kerkorian, were all high school drop outs. Steve Jobs and Bill Gates dropped out of college. Clearly, they continued to learn and educate themselves, through trial and error, outside of the traditional school system.

Your goal and job as a student of life should be just that – to learn and grow. Look at any kind of challenge as another opportunity to discover yourself.

Prepping For Tests

Let's remember the larger picture and the more important general process you should use to prepare for traditional written tests. First off, your approach to the class and your education in general will dictate how much "study" time you'll need. If you are practicing good habits of work and mind by calling yourself to task on a regular basis, raising your hand when you're confused, seeking answers to your questions regularly, following through thoroughly if you have to miss class, budgeting your time wisely, and using your learning strengths by tapping into specific strategies, then the amount of review time you need will probably be about a tenth of what you normally would spend if you weren't in those good habits. Also, the amount of stress you feel about the upcoming assessment will be dramatically reduced if not eliminated altogether.

Cramming

If you do have to cram, then information you cover will not make as much sense and you won't be able to retain or use it in the future nearly as effectively as if you were in those good habits. Cramming is not a sound pedagogical strategy for long-term learning. The only larger purpose it can serve is to train you to deal with high pressure situations in which you need to absorb lots of information quickly, which can be a useful process for certain professions such as lawyers, which is probably why law school isn't a pedagogically

146

sound environment either.

However, that being said, we all live, busy, complex lives. Everyone finds themselves in a situation, hopefully a rare one, where they will have to cram. If you are in a position where you're extremely behind in a subject with an exam quickly approaching, here are some pragmatic tips you can use.

- Imagine you're down to your last 24 hours before a major content-driven exam in history or science and you're completely unprepared. You need to absorb information at a fast rate. How you decide to spend every moment of free time you have within that 24-hour time frame is crucial and you cannot skip on sleep. Numerous studies support the fact that you retain so much more information with at least 6 hours of sleep and perform horribly under high pressure situations with less sleep. So, sleeping is part of your success equation.

- Find an environment that is conducive to focus and concentration. Very often, this is not where you live or in your dorm, but more like a library, coffee shop (I'm a huge fan of Starbucks myself, where I'm writing this book as I type) or any quiet space away from distractions and urges.

- Eliminate temptations that pull your focus away by turning off obvious culprits such as online chat forums, cell phones, TV, etc. unless you're using those as a learning tool to understand content.

- Never study while you're in bed. I repeat, never study while you're in your bed. Studying in bed limits your sustainable concentration because you have a conscious and subconscious association with bed as being a place to relax, sleep and recover (among other things). You also don't have the space, resources or ability to get on your feet to walk and think which is critical for so many learners. Lastly, it will negatively affect the quality of sleep you do get which will hurt your focus the next day.

When you have found a good place to park yourself and work, you first need to figure out the major points of what you'll need to know for that big test the next day. Do not get hung up on small details. What are the major areas that were emphasized in class? What are the section headings in the chapters you're responsible for in your text? What are the main points you can extract from your notes? Once you have the main points down, then you should tap into your own personal toolbox to absorb that information. It will vary from person to person depending on your innate strengths. If you're even relatively high in interpersonal intelligence, then I highly suggest finding a peer to study with. Just make sure that peer is as focused and serious about preparing for the exam as you are. It helps to be in the trenches with someone in this particular situation rather than to go at it all alone. Also, you do not have to spend your entire time together discussing the content. You can spend part of the time working independently while you're together and then regroup to discuss.

Be intelligent with how you budget your study time together and gauge your progress. If it's not beneficial, you should be flexible enough to make the necessary changes to take full advantage of your valuable time.

If you can't find a peer to prepare with, either in person or online, you can still achieve your desired outcome, which is to ace that exam. Again, the same strategies you've discovered when you're learning material in general apply when you're trying to cram, so tap into the "cram" learning strategies that coincide with your learning style the most. If you're high on the linguistic scale, reading your notes out loud is a must. It makes no sense to simply read your notes silently when you can hit three stimuli instead in the same amount of time by reading, speaking and listening.

Furthermore, use your recording function on your phone or computer while you say those notes. Listening back to your recorded voice will have a huge impact on your auditory senses which will help you retain more information than simply reading alone.

Another good technique you can use if you're high on the linguistic or logical-mathematical spectrum is writing and rewriting. That specific cram technique is really helpful when you write your notes with the purpose of trimming down the information down to the essentials. Not only does it help you identify what's really important, but the mere process of writing itself helps the information seep into your brain at a faster rate. If you continue the process of rewriting those notes again and again with the goal of trimming down the information to the bare essentials every time, you'll find that you're still able to recall details that you didn't write down in your latest version because you had to consciously omit them the last time you wrote. By consciously omitting, you're actually calling attention to it. It's almost like reverse psychology because by forcing yourself to eliminate pieces of information as you continue to rewrite, you're remembering them more.

If you're more visual-spatial, then you absolutely should outline and/or cluster your information. Outlining techniques can vary greatly, but they should all take advantage of your predisposition to absorb information by seeing it in some sort of patterned connection using symbols, pictures and colors along with an organizational hierarchy such as arrows, circles, boxes, roman numerals, numbers, and/or letters. By outlining your notes you're achieving the same outcome as in the writing-rewriting technique. You're actively identifying important information.

Try creating several different outlines such as a concept map, traditional outline with roman numerals and/or a picture outline to help you tap into different facets of your visual senses. Clustering or "chunking" information is a process in which you group related terms and ideas under one concept. It serves the visual learner even more if you create a color code or symbol that goes with the concept, such as different color note cards or colored pencils.

Take A Break

No matter what technique you're using, it's simply not sustainable to be studying hard for hours on end without a break. Many studies have shown that applying the 50-10 rule is the most effective work-break system. Simply put, stay focused and study hard for 50 minutes, then take a 10-minute break. Then start another 50-minute study cycle and so on and so on. I suggest using the timer or stopwatch function on your cell phone. Applying an official timer, rather than estimating, will remind you that you're on the clock and should be putting forth your best work. It also serves you well psychologically because you don't need to keep checking the time to see when the next break is coming. In addition, it instills in your mind that a break is coming, so it encourages you to put your best effort forward while you are working.

When your break does come, do not spend it taking in new information on social media, news reports or email. Your brain is constantly relinquishing memories to create the needed room for new information. If you inundate and distract your brain with new information while you're on your break, you can be sacrificing the information you're working so hard to retain. Instead, move your body and stretch, walk, do some deep breathing, get some fresh air, a drink of water or a light snack.

Speaking of snacks, it's hard to concentrate when you're hungry. Your brain needs blood sugar just to think. If you're hungry, you should take time to eat. However, be careful not to overeat. It can be just as damaging to eat too much food because it can create the lethargy that comes with a "food coma." Eat until your satiated, not until you're really "full."

Lastly, toward the end of your "cram" session, try to create a mock test situation. The context in which you learn something can have a big impact on your ability to recall what you learned. It's the same reason why the actors described in the chapter on kinesthetic memory were able to remember their lines from a play they did a year previously. They were able to remember through movement and the context in which they originally learned them. So why not create the context in which you'll need to recall information on your test?

Practice Tests

I often have students practice an exercise in class, in which they create their own test questions (essay, short answer, multiple choice, matching, etc.) based on the information we're covering. Interestingly, on average, students are able to anticipate approximately 90% of the actual material that will be on the exam!

The process of just writing the questions that challenge your higher order thinking skills will force you to really analyze what you know and don't know before you even take your own exam. I don't suggest spending a lot of effort writing time-consuming questions such as the perfect multiple choice or matching question along with answer choices that even include a trick answer. Instead, look online where you can often find multiple choice and matching, as well as short answer and essay questions. (Just make sure to self-tailor the latter.) In fact, some teachers actually research and modify multiple choice questions that they find online, so chances are you might be working with the same questions that actually appear on your real test!

Once you've put together a practice test, sit down and answer the questions under the same conditions in which you'll be taking the exam the next day. In addition to analyzing what you know and don't know, it will give you a psychological advantage of familiarity and confidence when you sit down to take the real test the next day.

Remember that just like any other skill, practice makes perfect. A test, particularly a standardized one, is really a test in test taking itself. Huge tutoring companies such as Kaplan, Princeton Review, Tutor.com, etc., wouldn't exist if that wasn't true. Therefore, the encouraging news is you will get better at taking tests as you get older simply because you will have more and more practice at it. You'll probably find that by the time you're a senior in high school or freshman in college, you are skilled at specific techniques such as eliminating possible wrong choices on multiple choice questions. Choices that have "always" or "never" in them, for example, are rarely correct because there is usually always an exception to the rule.

When you analyze the SAT, each section can be broken down into three progressive sections – easy, medium and hard. However, you don't get any more points by answering a multiple-choice question in the hard section as you do in the easy one. Therefore, a good strategy is to make sure you have all the questions in the easy and medium category correct before you dedicate all your time toward trying to answer a hard question. Acquiring points in those first two sections are worth the same amount, but a lot easier.

In addition, the SAT used to penalize students for getting a question wrong, but not for omitting a question. Therefore, it was advantageous to skip questions rather than flat out guess on a question that you had no clue as to the answer. Students had been known to bring up their SAT score by hundreds of points simply by skipping questions. That rule since has changed, but it obviously points out the fact that test-taking strategies can be learned and utilized, regardless of what the content of the exam is about.

Negotiating Your Grade

Here's one last statement about grades resulting from assessments, whether it's at the end of a big exam, a grading term, or the whole year. **Most teachers won't like to admit it, but grades can be negotiated.** Yes, that is correct. With the right approach, you can negotiate your grade with your teachers, department chairs and administrators. I have seen countless examples of students getting extra points back on tests, final exams, at the end of a grading period, year and even missing work excused.

It's ironic that an area meant to be completely objective can become fairly subjective, but it is true. How does a student get the leverage to negotiate grades? The reputation you've established throughout your time in that class and at the school will be the leading factor. If you can honestly say that you've put forth your best effort, were punctual, extremely conscientious with all assignments and supportive and friendly with both your peers and teachers, then you already have a lot of power. The more you've fallen short on the latter, the more you will lose your ability to bargain.

When should you try to negotiate grades? It really depends on the teacher you're dealing with. With some teachers, simply taking that initiative alone will prompt them to possibly make an exception. With others, they might resist. Do not let that stop you from trying. If you're dealing with a teacher who you believe might be resistant, then I would get in the habit of only making the attempt when it will have a strong impact on the outcome of your grade overall.

Your opportunities to negotiate might be limited depending on who you're trying to negotiate with, so know who you're dealing with and choose your times wisely. If you try to negotiate with your teacher too many times, chances are you might have less room to do it as time goes on. In addition, if you choose to do it in situations that didn't have a big impact on your grade, then you might have less of a chance to do it at important times when you really need it. Therefore, if it's a few points on a quiz, it's probably not worth it.

Please note, I am not referring to a situation in which an actual mistake was made on an assessment, such as an answer you marked correctly that was mistakenly marked wrong. I'm referring to situations where you made a legitimate mistake and lost points, but are trying to get those points back anyway. First off, I suggest scheduling an appointment with your teacher so you can speak with him/her in person. It will work to your benefit to be direct and get right to the point. You should be prepared to support your reasons for the grade bump you're requesting with specific details. Since it can sometimes be an uncomfortable conversation for students to have, you should map out the major points of what you'd like to say before you meet.

Students higher on the interpersonal intelligence scale will have an easier time with this process, but regardless of where you fall on that intelligence spectrum, I suggest setting up a mock conversation. Use your strengths to either write, speak or act out exactly what you want to say and how you want to say it. Role playing is a great way to prep for the real conversation as well.

Once you finally do have your meeting, remember to keep an open mind and to accept any outcome. Despite your preparation and best efforts, your teacher might say no if they feel your request is too unreasonable. Remember – as long as you're being polite, professional and courteous, then you really cannot go wrong.

MR. PFAFF'S TAKEAWAYS:

- Practice strong, consistent habits of work and mind to learn better and avoid heavy cram sessions.

- Tests (especially standardized) are often a skill in test taking itself, regardless of content.

- Eliminate distractions and choose the right environment when studying.

- If forced to cram, use the 50-10 rule, along with rewriting and clustering techniques.

- Grades can be negotiated.

CHAPTER 11 Anxiety

"You can't stop the waves, but you can learn to surf."

– Jon Kabat-Zinn, professor of medicine, creator of the Stress Reduction clinic and the Center for Mindfulness in Medicine

To understand how to manage anxiety, we first have to understand the nature of it. Anxiety is defined as "a feeling of worry, nervousness, or unease, typically about an imminent event or something with an uncertain outcome." Think about that again for a moment, "a feeling of worry or unease about something with an uncertain outcome."

It is human nature to want to feel in control of our lives and all the events that unfold in them. While I do believe in the law of attraction and that we evoke into our lives that which we are thinking, feeling and desiring, nobody can predict exactly what will happen. If that were possible, we'd be seeing more psychics at the horse races.

Therefore, the key to managing anxiety, no matter how much of it you're feeling, is to recognize what is within your control and what isn't. Once you have that figured out, your job is to put your focus and energy onto what you can control. Also, learning to embrace and take pleasure in the process and journey over the outcome and destination will turn anxiety into engagement and nervousness into pleasure.

Let's take an honest look at what is actually in our control. In general, we can control how we prepare and how we react. We cannot control what happens to us. Try this exercise. Identify something in your life that, either in the past or present, has caused or is presently causing you anxiety. Create a simple list with two columns, a T-chart works great. Write down the event, place or person at the top of the list of things that are making you nervous. On the left, list all the details about it which are NOT within your control. In the right-hand column, list the details about it that ARE within your control. Skim both columns over quickly, then put a big "X" through that left-hand column. Eliminate it, cross it out, forget about it. Shift all your attention to the right side.

If you practice this simple exercise regularly, you'll notice your right-hand column keeps getting longer and longer than the left, which is evidence that your focus is shifting to the right (pun intended) place. For example, I used to get really nervous before track and cross-country races I ran in middle school, high school and even college. Toward the end of my running career at Penn State and afterward when I was racing for Reebok Boston, that nervousness subsided a lot. Part of the reason was the recognition of what was within my power and what wasn't.

The other reason was my willingness to prepare. For my particular T chart, one of the factors I might have listed is obvious – how well I run in the race. On the left-hand column of my particular list – the things that are not within my control – I might list items such as: how fast other athletes run in the race, the weather, the time of day, or the type of track. Putting my focus on any of those details was a waste of my time and energy. On the right-hand side of my list I'd have details such as: making sure I warm up and stretch really well before the race, getting off the line fast and with control, staying loose and relaxed while running, being conscious of not getting boxed in, maintaining good running form, having fun and competing to win. Putting my focus on the right-hand side became very productive for me because it gave me a place to put my energy; it gave me a process, a way of doing things that became a familiar friend. In fact, it soon took up so much of my concentration that I didn't have time to think about other things that could potentially make me nervous.

Let's use another example. Perhaps you have a classmate, teammate, coworker or boss you don't get along with and you perceive this person as anxiety causing. On the left-hand side of your column, you might have details such as: what they say, what they do, how they react to the things you say and do, etc. Now you know these things are out of your control, right? Wouldn't it be really freeing to put a big "X" through all those things? Just let them go! It is a waste of your mental energy, valuable focus time, and peace of mind. Instead, focus on the right-hand side of your list such as: what you consistently do, how you react to what that person says and does, how you're going to consciously employ calming techniques if you get agitated, angry or anxious. **We can only control our own actions, not the actions of others. While we all know this fact, some of us need to constantly remind ourselves.**

Doing Your Homework

The other big factor concerning the situation that's causing you anxiety is the amount of preparation you've put in to deal with it. Think about an activity you enjoy that you're really good at. It could be anything. Pick something easy such as doing accents, dancing, playing an instrument, or a fun hobby such as twirling a fidget spinner, playing a video game, or repeating the lyrics to your favorite song. If a teacher told you they're going to test you on how well you do that activity, chances are high you'd be able to handle it pretty well. Sure, you might get temporarily nervous when you hear the word "test," but the mere fact that you've logged so many hours doing that particular activity would give you a quiet, calm confidence to tackle whatever test that teacher threw at you. Why should any other situation be different?

Nothing is worth giving up or taking away your peace of mind. If any kind of situation, event or person is taking that peace away from you, reclaim it through preparation and intense focus on what's in your control.

Focus And Be Productive

Have you ever seen an Olympic athlete get ready for an event? Take a moment to really watch the level of focus and concentration they have before a track event like the 100m, a swimming event such as the 50m freestyle, or a boxing match. Even if you wanted, you wouldn't be able to break their concentration. That level of focus and confidence only comes from countless hours, days, weeks, months and years of intense training.

These athletes were able to obtain that confidence through preparation. But you don't have to be an Olympic athlete to claim your confidence. If you have nervous energy, put it somewhere. Don't just sit idly and continue to be nervous. Use that nervous energy toward productivity. The mere act of doing something rather than nothing is empowering in itself. Progress of any kind is motivating, reassuring and productive. By taking some sort of directed action you will be making progress and will enjoy all the benefits that come with it. As TV actor/director Richard Kline once said, "Confidence is preparation. Everything else is beyond your control." The longer you study, train, practice, and mentally rehearse for anything challenging in your life, the more confident you will be not only in that situation, but all others as well.

American psychologist Julian Rotter first introduced the idea of "locus of control" back in the 1950s. Much like Carol Dweck's explanation of a growth vs. fixed mindset, Rotter's theory taps into an individual's perception of themselves and the world. According to this idea, a student with an internal locus of control or growth mindset will see the results of an exam as something that is within their own control (i.e. the way they prepared, study strategies they used, amount of time and effort they put in, etc.). A student with an external locus of control or fixed mindset will see the results of an exam as something not within their control (i.e. their teacher gives exams that are too difficult, their schedule didn't allow them to study, the pressures of life caused them to become unfocused, etc.). It's the same event for those two types of students, but two completely different perspectives.

"My anxieties have anxieties!" – Charlie Brown

Retrain Your Mind

Part of the problem with people who have high levels of anxiety is they fail to differentiate between productive thoughts that can serve them and nagging thoughts that give them no advantage. They can't seem to stop their mind from jumping toward thoughts that are not within their control. If you're one of those people who consistently has useless worries that don't serve you, then you need to retrain your mind to focus your internal locus of control toward thoughts that serve. A specific technique to practice in order to do this is meditation.

There is a trend among the world's most successful people: they all practice some form of meditation. Why is meditation beneficial? It trains your mind to direct your thoughts toward only that which serves. Much like a boxer who's repeatedly trained to block, dodge, and move around punches to find his or her own opening to strike, **meditation trains the mind to block, dodge and move around negative thoughts to find your pathway toward productive thinking**. But don't take my word for it, take a look at the 47 studies analyzed in JAMA (*Journal of the American Medical Association*) that support the positive effects of meditation, or studies conducted at countless universities and hospitals all over the country.

Being a Bostonian at heart, a few of my favorite studies are the 2013 study on the incredible improvement of patients diagnosed with DSM-IV (Diagnosed Generalized Anxiety Disorder) at Massachusetts General Hospital. I also like the Harvard affiliated researchers who discovered continuous meditation physically changes the brain's gray matter. Lastly, a smaller, more recent study conducted here in Southern California, supported the fact that regular meditation was more beneficial than vacation, which really resonated with me. Oh yea, did I also mention meditation enhances your memory, focus, creativity, decision making skills, immune system, cardiovascular system, can reduce physical pain, mental pain, stress, addictions and even bring you closer to enlightenment? Let's take a look at some meditative techniques.

Many different forms and ideas about meditation exist, but the end goal is the same – to calm and quiet the mind and raise consciousness. You'll obviously need to find a quiet space and eliminate all distractions to meditate. If you're alone and trying it for the first time, you have a plethora of free guided tours online that walk you through it. Try some free apps such as Headspace, MyCalmBeat, Calm, Buddhify or Smiling Mind. Also, free guided tours on chopra.com, mindfulness-solution.com and even YouTube will work great.

In the end, you'll be getting the same general advice, which is to direct your attention on your breath, body, or sensation and to let whatever other thoughts that arise in that moment to pass by. Your body can be in a comfortable laying, sitting, or standing position, but also can be done with movement, whether it's yoga, walking, or exercising of almost any kind. The key is to center yourself and eliminate distractions which pull you away from that center. By continually practicing that technique, you're strengthening your minds ability to direct your thoughts toward what you want, toward what's productive.

If you're a beginner, concentration meditation (versus mindful meditation) is the best place to start. Find a quiet space and sit or stand in a comfortable position. My foot tends to fall asleep if I'm in a cross-legged seated position, so I prefer to stand. Hand position can vary greatly depending on your body position, but try resting them on your knees if you're kneeling, palms open and upward on your thighs if you're sitting or simply at your side if you're standing. Start with small increments so set a timer on your phone for 5-10 minutes. Check in with your body and mind and allow your whole body to relax, including your eyes. I prefer to close my eyes, but you don't have to, as long as your eyes aren't shifting around the room taking in new stimuli.

Choose what your concentration point will be. I've found the easiest starting point is to simply focus on my own breath. If you choose the same, breathe deeply – in through your nose and out through your mouth. Concentrate solely on that.

Your concentration point, however, can be many things, such as an object, word, phrase, place in your body, sound, mental image, etc. Don't choose anything that stimulates too much of a reaction such as excitement or boredom. A common object that practitioners often focus on, for example, is a candle. Common words or phrases are often from a sacred text and resonate with you personally. Common mental images include symbols, places and elements that have personal meaning. In the end, however, it's never about what you choose as your concentration point, it's about training your mind to focus.

As you focus on your chosen concentration point, other thoughts will begin to emerge. That's okay. Simply notice them and allow them to pass by, and then put your focus back on what your original concentration point is. It's much more beneficial to start off trying to meditate for 5-10 minutes every day then to try to do it once a week for an hour.

Keep in mind many forms of meditation exist. If you're more of an active person perhaps something with movement such as Yoga, Tai Chi, Chi Gong (Qigong) or a simple walk outside will suit you more. The same principles of a focus on the breath, with deep, controlled breathing, and heightened body awareness apply when you're engaged with any one of those activities, although you might have to be more deliberate about it if you're out for a walk. These activities have the same therapeutic benefits of meditation, such as reduced stress, anxiety, tension and can even ease symptoms of depression.

I was personally introduced to a regular practice of Chi Gong when I started studying Kung Fu about a year ago. After a few weeks, I started noticing benefits such as increased focus, energy and general calmness. I started getting up early every morning to practice Chi Gong for about 20 minutes before I went to work. The results have been astounding. While I've always been a high-energy person, my focus has often been dissipated into many different areas. The main result I've personally received from this regular Chi Gong practice is an increased ability to direct my energy into an intended direction without diversion. Therefore, I can easily say the result has been directed focus, which in turn, is increased focus.

A good analogy is harnessing the sun's power with a magnifying glass. While that sunlight does have a wealth of energy, it doesn't have the power to burn through a piece of wood until you know how to harness that energy by using a magnifying glass as a tool. Your tool is meditation and it can empower you to burn through any obstacle in your way.

Progressive relaxation, visualization and autogenic relaxation are also good techniques for relaxation and focus. I'm a big fan of progressive relaxation because I was first introduced to it back at Penn State University and it's one of those easy to maintain practices that just stuck with me. The technique involves moving through general muscle groups in your body, contracting and relaxing them one by one. You can start at the bottom or top of your body, but I like to start with my toes. I contract them for about five seconds and then relax for 30 seconds. Then I move up to my calves, quadriceps, hamstring, buttocks, stomach, arms, chest, shoulders, jaw muscle and forehead.

This specific technique can bring about more body awareness, in general, to let you know when you're tense, which you might not even be aware of. It also shifts your attention onto your body, training the mind to focus.

Autogenic (auto meaning "self" so it comes from within you) relaxation is another technique in which the practitioner self-instructs their own body to follow a simple set of relaxation instructions. They commonly instruct their body to control regulatory mechanisms such as breathing, heart rate and body temperature, but it can also be on relaxing any physical sensations you might feel in your body, such as the shoulders, stomach or legs.

Visualization is another great one. With this technique, the practitioner takes a visual journey to a peaceful place with a focus on taking that environment in with as many senses as you can. What you hear, see, smell, feel and taste are all important. Since my happy place is the beach at Breezy Point, New York, I picture myself walking alone as I feel the warm sun on my face and the sand beneath my toes. I hear the ocean waves rolling in as the seagulls call in the distance. I smell the breeze off the ocean and taste the salt water in the mist of the air. The more details you take in with those memory senses, the more real it can become and the larger the therapeutic effect it can have.

Mindfulness is a term that is widely used today and sometimes debated. Formal mindfulness is very much the same focus as the other meditative techniques we discussed – attention to breath, body and sensations. Informal mindfulness simply brings conscious attention to your mind's interpretation of everyday life. According to Jon Kabat-Zinn, professor of medicine and creator of the stress reduction clinic at the University of Massachusetts Medical School, "mindfulness means paying attention in a particular way; on purpose, in the present moment, and non-judgmentally."

When you start to analyze what Kabat really means by this, it's revealed that we carry tremendous baggage filled with opinions and bias about everything. Very often, our bag of opinions causes us to misanalyze present situations, giving our rigid interpretation limited options, such as good or bad. Being aware of our own judgments allows us to see not only when that's happening, which is pretty much all the time, but it allows us to better experience life without automatic judgment. The benefit is a more accurate analysis of our present life, which for the majority of the time, isn't as bad or as anxiety-provoking as our rigid biased interpretation might make it seem.

In summary, **remember that you alone own the power of your mind**. No matter what your situation, innate genetics, socio-economic class or ethnicity, you own your mind. Understanding and using that power will not only equip you to cope and conquer anxiety-ridden situations, but it will enable you to achieve anything you want in your life. The tools for you to unlock the doors of your choice are available, but nobody else can use them for you. That power is only discovered if the tool of choice is wielded in your hands alone. As author Pavel Stoyanov states: ***"The major cause of stress is the inability of people to discover their true nature. Discover your gifts, follow them and you will never feel stressed."***

MR. PFAFF'S TAKEAWAYS

- Thorough preparation helps to greatly reduce anxiety.

- Do not worry or waste energy on that which is not within your control.

- Employ a regular meditative practice into your life.

CHAPTER 12 Life Applications – Not Just For Grades

"Education is not the learning of facts, but the training of the mind to think."
— Albert Einstein, scientist

What's your purpose in life? What are you passionate about? What do you really want to do? I know, those are tough questions to answer. However, finding the answers to those questions can make all the difference in your happiness and quality of life.

In order to begin to find the answers to those questions, you have to look inside yourself and really learn to think. In other words, your education is the key to your life. Yes, life will always give us gentle nudges, or an outright push, to reevaluate, rethink and restructure our thoughts. If you're able to recognize life's nudges as signs toward ultimate fulfillment, then nothing will get in the way of the enjoyment and happiness you deserve.

Take a moment to think about the times you've felt the best about yourself. Chances are, no matter what you're thinking of, it involved helping someone in some direct or indirect way. Whether you were thinking about a close friendship, a romantic relationship, a big accomplishment, or just a hearty laugh, those feelings of love, laughter and joy are contagious. If you're feeling them, then you're spreading them as well. It's why they say laughter is contagious. Those feelings are gifts, not only to enjoy for yourself but to share with others.

I personally believe we discover this truth in life more and more as we move closer toward self-actualization. One can only get there by learning the truth – that there is no greater gift then giving. The best kind of giving is that of yourself, whether it be knowledge, love, awareness, kindness, skills, patience or a combination of these and many others.

If you're a fan of *The Secret*, the decade old bestselling book by Rhonda Byrne, I'm sure you've read that you can't really take care of anyone until you take care of yourself. Yes, it does seem selfish when you first hear that statement, but if you can't swim and keep yourself above water, how could you help someone who is drowning in the ocean?

Self-actualization

If you can make the connection between the development of self and your increasing power to help others, then you're truly on a continuous path of a joyful, exciting, rewarding life full of love, laughter and happiness. The happiest people in life are those who have become self-actualized. **Self-actualization can be described as complete contentment and harmony with the way you live your life due to your own self-knowledge, which you use to motivate, inspire and achieve things for yourself and others.** That knowledge is used to cultivate loving, fulfilling relationships, and that knowledge is used to find true meaning and purpose in the world in which you live. I believe we all have this ability to become self-actualized and to draw to us that which we desire for ourselves and others. It's our responsibility to put in the necessary measures to self-discover in order to get there.

Case in point. When I first started writing this book approximately six months ago, I referenced an actor named Robert Patrick in chapter 3 ("finding the right tool") to illustrate my point about the dynamic nature of motivation and how you can adapt yourself to cultivate inspiration in any situation and at any time. Just last week, which was over half a year since I first wrote those words, I received news about my first big network booking of 2018 in a show called *Scorpion* on CBS. It was my first big TV booking in quite some time. While I was vaguely familiar with the show, I didn't know any of the actors in it. When the producers sent my sides, I was shocked, not only to see who the actors were that were in it, but whom my scene was actually with. As it turned out, I had booked a phenomenal scene with the T-1000 himself, Robert Patrick!

My eyes swelled with tears of joy when I first saw this because for me, it was clear evidence of the law of attraction at work. You'll never know exactly how the universe will come back to meet you with the energy you put out there, but it will meet you.

Furthermore, while on set, I hit it off amazingly well with Robert and the director who were both incredible. However, I also met an actor who was my stand-in that day. He was disenchanted with the whole business. He was a struggling a lot with the lack of opportunity in the industry (any actor on earth can relate to that) because he wasn't getting enough auditions and opportunities to work. He was considering moving to Canada for the potential of more job opportunities. He started asking me questions about how I booked that particular job, where I studied, etc.

We ended up talking for well over an hour after I wrapped. I listened to his struggles and offered my own personal experiences and insight to hopefully help him figure out his own path. When I was driving home that night after a great day on set, I realized part of my purpose was to help him to the best of my ability. We are all meant to serve, help and provide for others in some way, shape or form. On that particular day, that was my way.

Chances are you've heard, at some point in your life, that "happiness comes from within." That happiness comes from excitement, excitement from knowing yourself, your own passions, desires and endless potential. It's so important to know that this kind of self-discovery and reliance can be realized in what might seem to be the bleakest of situations. In fact, the most powerful self-discoveries, gifts and blessings bestowed on us as a human race often rise from places of pain, adversity and strife. Without prejudice, we would have had no Dr. Martin Luther King, without war we would have had no Mahatma Gandhi, and without sickness and disease we would have had no Mother Teresa. Those three commonly known examples are among millions of heroes. Those heroes potentially live in us.

> Did you hear about the rose that grew from a crack in the concrete?
> Proving nature's law is wrong, it learned to walk without having feet.
> Funny it seems, but by keeping its dreams, it learned to breathe fresh air.
> Long live the rose that grew from concrete, when no one else ever cared."
> — Tupac Shakur

I grew up in North Jersey and attended a beautifully diverse public high school in Hackensack. That experience served me well in life and provided me more of what I'd call an education than any kind of schooling. When I reflect on that education back then, I'm constantly reminded that you experience the life you choose.

A friend and teammate I had my freshman year didn't make it to his sophomore year because he was shot in the head. Another friend and teammate on that same team was shot five times in the back and killed the year after I graduated high school. Several additional friends, with whom I spent a lot of my childhood and high school time, ended up in jail for over a decade. When I think about the painful experiences and situations these specific friends suffered, I'm reminded not only of the necessity but of the responsibility we all have to be the best versions of ourselves.

Your best versions can only be seen when you have the courage to look in the mirror early on, to self- analyze and self-discover. When you do this, you gain true insight and education that sets you toward your personal purpose. And with that purpose you can overcome any obstacle and shine light on any darkness. While we all have different innate strengths and abilities, we also have one common truth – we are all inherently good.

Have you ever seen a baby, whether from Africa, Asia, India or the U.S., whether they are suffering from a disease or not, who doesn't experience joy from a warm embrace from their mother or caregiver? Have you ever seen a toddler care about the way another toddler looks, or their socio-economic status, religious beliefs or politics before they decide to play with one another? If you observe closely, you'll also see babies, toddlers and children displaying empathy if another one around them is crying or suffering in some way. That human condition is our true universal essence. It's the way you perceive and process the outside world and experiences that can pull us away from that human condition.

How you see the world is largely dependent on how you see and know yourself. In order to do that, you need the courage to look. Through self-analysis, any kind of fear, ignorance, adversity and pain can be overcome. Even suffering will have a positive meaning if you know yourself well enough to learn from it and even use it. Very often, when you look at people with a lot of knowledge and support to offer others, it's because they've suffered themselves. So those negative experiences can serve not only your own betterment, but the betterment of those around you. **Education is the key to overcoming pain and suffering and to experiencing and spreading the happiness you and those around you deserve.**

My Deer Journey

When I was 20 years old, I had a painful experience, which helped shape my perspective in life for the better. It resonated so profoundly that it took a very long time for me to make sense of the event and get comfortable enough to share with others. Looking back now, I realize the purpose behind that event was for me to learn certain inevitable truths that govern our universe and to live my life with purpose.

I was driving home from a 4th of July weekend getaway that a college friend had for a bunch of our teammates on the Penn State track team. It was so much fun that I would have stayed through the entire weekend and left Monday afternoon, but I had to be at work early Monday morning. I was working as a lifeguard at a health club that summer.

So, I got in as much time with my friends as I could before I got in the car Sunday night for the four-hour drive home back to my hometown in New Jersey. I wasn't drinking alcohol and I was aware and awake for the long ride home. It was, however, dark outside.

As I was driving along the dark highway on 380 East, it was hard to see far ahead. The highway wasn't lit very well and I drove an old car that didn't have the brightest headlights. As I was driving in the left lane of the highway, a deer suddenly ran in front of my car out of nowhere. I didn't have any time to react and slammed on the breaks, but my car still hit the deer. The deer went flying off into the distance all the way to the right side of the highway as my car skidded off to the left off the highway. Instantly, I got out of my car to see if the deer was okay, but it wasn't. The deer gently lowered its head down onto the concrete as if its soul had left its body.

A wave of devastation hit me. I've never killed anything in my entire life before that moment and I was now responsible for taking the life of this beautiful, peaceful animal. Needless to say, I felt horrible. Alone in the dark I stood there staring at the deer across the highway and began to cry. I felt an instinctive need to walk across that dark highway to get close to that deer, put my hand on it and say a prayer. But as an 18-wheeler Mac truck sped by, I realized it was too dangerous to walk across all those lanes of that dark interstate highway.

So, I stood there alone, in the dark, as feelings of pain, shame and blame took over. After spending a long time by myself, I finally decided to say a prayer for that deer from where I stood. I prayed that the deer didn't feel any pain. I wondered about the soul of that animal and if animals experience an afterlife. Lastly, I asked God to forgive me. Finally, I got back into my car to continue my drive home. Before I started, however, I decided to put on my seatbelt. Now I know this was a horrible habit, but before that night, I had never worn my seatbelt. It just wasn't a habit that I was in and the cars in those days didn't beep or ding if you didn't wear your seatbelt. But this particular night, after that horrifying event, I decided to put it on.

I began the drive down 380 East again as I looked for signs for 80 East to make my way home. As I was driving, I kept thinking about the deer, and at the same time, I remember subconsciously pulling the chest strap on my seatbelt so it tightened around the waist. I didn't know why I was doing it. I just was. Eventually, I got to the Delaware Water Gap, and I was about 30 minutes into NJ on route 80 and what do you think happened? What do you think the chances of hitting two deer in one night are? I am not kidding or exaggerating. Another big deer with antlers jumped in front of my car into my lane. Again, I had no time to react. I slammed on my brakes and my car hit the deer. From the impact of hitting the dear, my car jolted into the adjacent right lane on the highway and into the lane of an 18-

wheeler Mac truck. That 18-wheeler Mac truck ran over my entire car and took off into the air, flying airborne off the Interstate 80 highway.

The sound of the crash was deafening and the impact sent my car spinning violently and uncontrollably down the highway. Broken glass hit me in the face from every angle as I bounced back and forth in my car seat, but the whole time, the seatbelt held me in. Finally, my car stopped spinning around and I didn't know if I was even on the highway anymore. I shook my head and broken glass came falling out of my hair.

A moment later, I realized I was still on the highway when I saw in the rear view mirror another two mac trucks coming straight toward my car from behind. There was not enough time to run out of the car so I just grasped onto the steering wheel for dear life.

At the last second, both Mack trucks split off in opposite directions around my car, just narrowly missing me. I felt my car shake as they flew by. Finally, I took off my seatbelt, got out of the car, and ran to the truck driver to see if he was okay.

When I got to the driver side door of his truck, I immediately knocked on the window. I noticed him inside just staring in shock. He lowered the window and I asked him if he was okay. He said, "Yeah, but the driver." I told him that I was the driver. He took a look at me stunned and said, in a good-ole-boy accent, "God damn boy, I thought you was dead."

But I wasn't dead. In fact, I wasn't even hurt. In that moment, I looked back at my car on the highway and it looked like a smooshed can. Every window was broken, the car was crushed, every tire was busted. I couldn't even get back into the car if I wanted, yet I somehow came out of it without a scratch.

When state troopers arrived to the scene minutes later, one of them told me that he's been a state trooper for over 25 years and have never seen anything like it. He said he couldn't believe I was alive, let alone not even injured. After inspecting the front of my car, that same trooper said to me, "that was a huge deer... you've got blood and deer fur on both the front right and left sides of your car, it covers the whole width." Of course, I wasn't about to tell him that the blood on the right side of the car was actually from the first deer I hit that night; he would have thought I was purposely going after them!

After EMT arrived to the scene and inspected both the truck driver and me, I was finally driven to a pay phone to call my family (this was before everyone was carrying around their own cell phone). After a while, I was able to get in touch with my mom. She's always been a very spiritual person and said to me that she had a feeling something was wrong that night, so said a prayer that I get home safely. Whether you want to call it a spirit, an energy, or a prayer, that first deer saved my life.

My first reaction on the day after that car crash was to immediately get back into my regular routine. I even took my normal training run the next day as if nothing had happened less than 12 hours earlier. Besides some slight whiplash in my neck, I felt fine. However, after taking more time to really reflect on that incident, the conclusion I repeatedly came to was that my transition simply wasn't meant to happen that night.

The few people I've shared this story with sometimes ask me if I was scared when the crash happened. When I think back about it, the truth is, I wasn't. For some reason, I felt safe. As strange as it sounds, I felt like there was a pressure, almost like a hand on my chest, pushing me back into my car seat so my body wouldn't slam into the steering wheel every time I bounced back and forth as my car repeatedly spun down that long dark highway. In that moment of chaos, for whatever reason, I felt protected.

Years later, a good friend and I were backpacking through Europe together. We were walking through the Louvre museum in France as I told him what happened the night of that car crash. He had never heard the story before since I wasn't at a place in my life where I was sharing it with a lot of people. He was engrossed in listening to what happened to me just as much as I was engrossed in telling him so we weren't noticing the artwork around us as we walked down the hallway. What I do remember is when I finished telling him what happened that night, we both noticed we were standing near a large statue of St. Michael with his hand on a deer.

I want to emphasize that I had never been a very religious person. In fact, I still don't consider myself to be religious. I am now full of faith and have a strong spiritual sense, but don't identify with any particular religion. When the car accident happened, I definitely wasn't engaged in a lot of self-contemplation at that time in my life. Who was I back then? An athlete who was pursuing a Bachelor of Science degree. Facts, pragmatism and hard physical and mental training was where I found my truth.

A part of me still has that same mentality today. I've now taught high school science full time for 15 years. I am not sharing what happened the night of my car accident to promote any kind of religion. However, I am saying that the events in our life can lead us to our own truth and purpose if we engage ourselves in deep, self-directed education. I am also saying that the power of prayer is real. We have overwhelming scientific evidence that supports this fact. Whatever you choose to call it, there is an energy that connects us all. Knowing yourself will help you interpret that energy and make sense of the events that happen in your life. More importantly, it will reveal meaning which can empower you to live life with purpose and help others.

I believe in science and I have a very strong faith that a higher power exists. To think that they are two opposing ideas is absurd. It doesn't matter what we choose to call the life force that binds living things, what matters is the recognition that we are all connected. I know for a fact that I didn't die that night because I'm on this earth to serve a purpose. We all have a purpose. That event that happened in my life was more than a gentle nudge, it was a violent crash to remind me of that truth. Through self-analysis, discovery, and developing the courage to do that which challenges us, we all can find enlightenment and a discovery of our purpose.

My hope is that this book has served you in some way and that it provides you with some specific tools which will help you to find your purpose. **Finding your purpose involves a commitment to your education, not necessarily your schooling.** The purpose of this book is to help you learn more effectively, to inspire you to be more self-reflective, and to prompt you to reach out and help others in need.

I am wishing you an abundance of success, fulfillment, love and joy in your academic, personal, physical and spiritual selves. I am wishing you success in life. Take good care and remember that if you ever feel yourself getting lost, look within yourself to find the way.

MR. PFAFF'S TAKEAWAYS

- Education is vital to overcome pain and suffering.

- You experience more joy in life, have more love to give, and form more meaningful relationships when you live your life with purpose.

- Use your own innate faculties to help others.

- The power of prayer is scientifically proven.

- Wear your seatbelt.

POSTWORD

Mike Pfaff has been teaching high school science for 15 years in both public and private school systems on both coasts. He's taught physiology, A.P., honors and general biology, honors and general physics and honors and general chemistry. His main areas of expertise are in physiology and biology. He's also taught educational psychology and public speaking at the college level as an adjunct professor for many years at Suffolk University.

Competing on an elite level in Track and Cross Country at the high school, college and post collegian level taught Mike a lot about the sources of motivation, value of leadership and necessity of teamwork. He was captain of his cross country and track team in high school before attending Penn State University on a NCAA Division 1 Track scholarship. He graduated from Penn State as captain of the cross country and track team before heading to Boston to continue running for an elite post collegian running team, Reebok Boston.

After three knee surgeries, Mike's running career ended and he directed that same passion, energy and mindset toward teaching. Mike was a two-time "teacher of the year" at South Boston High School (renamed Monument High School, one part of the South Boston Educational Complex). Even after making the decision to move out West,

Mike still maintains positive mentoring relationships with many of his former students from Boston.

In addition to teaching, Mike is also an actor and stuntman. You can see Mike on network and cable TV shows such as *Sons of Anarchy, Two Broke Girls, Scorpion, The Librarians, Deadliest Warrior* and *Fields of Valor*. You can also catch him in several leading and supporting roles on independent feature films that have landed distribution deals on major platforms.

The combination of teaching and acting has given Mike a powerful gateway toward empowering kids to find their own sources of passion, motivation and innate strengths. The reality that the art and science of learning can truly be applied and expressed when aligning what's in your heart with what you're choosing to do with your life inspired Mike to write his first book. It is the first book of a series of three.

TEACHER/TEACHER-TO-BE/PARENT GUIDE

Foreword to Parents:

A big kiss of death for a teacher is to teach, even on a subconscious level, with the understanding that all students can learn the same way they did. It's just as important for a parent to understand that truth, too. Yes, at times biological parents will quickly notice that their kids inherited certain faculties from one or both parents, but that doesn't mean all learning is best done in the same manner. Also, remember that your child's self-discoveries will continuously happen over the course of a lifetime. Therefore, it's never too late for them to start. By staying open minded, encouraging your child's own metacognition, and celebrating little breakthroughs they experience, you'll empower them to unravel the inner workings of their own mind. It's a precious gift and will serve them well their entire lives.

Most children don't understand that one of the healthiest conversations they can have with their teacher is how their own mind works, how they process information, and how they think they learn best. Most students automatically think they're supposed to understand everything being taught in class in the exact way the teacher is presenting and the way everyone else is learning. They dismiss the idea that another tactic might be more personally beneficial. This mindset allows school structure to limit the potential of their own mind. Your child can still flourish within that school structure, but will do so by leveraging different, specific, personal strategies. Encouraging them to use those strategies, to courageously discuss them with their teacher, and to always be aware of how their own mind is processing will empower them to continually evolve as learners.

In addition, numerous studies and overwhelming evidence support the fact that punishment of any kind is negative reinforcement that does nothing to change behavior in anyone, especially teenagers. In fact, not only is it ineffective, but it can be harmful to a child's development. The term discipline itself comes from the Latin root "discipulus," meaning pupil or to teach. As a parent, redefining what discipline really means can empower you to support your child's development in a more meaningful way. If you're serious about supporting a positive change in behavior, then use positive reinforcement.

Lastly, I've seen parents, especially in private schools, spend exorbitant amounts of money hiring tutors. While that can be helpful in certain situations, it should be used as a last resort. In addition, if a tutor is hired, part of that tutor's job is to empower your child to develop enough strong preparatory and management skills so that tutoring will no longer be needed. There is a larger price that is paid besides a tutor's hourly rate. The price is a level of apathy in a student that counteracts the challenging undertaking required of all students to truly flourish. An automatic default to tutors can rob your child of the necessary processes needed to reach their true potential.

If your child is struggling in any given class, they must reach out to the teacher of that individual class first. That single act in itself is a necessary life lesson, not an optional one. By the time a student is a freshman in high school, they should be doing this on their own regularly. How to do it might need to be demonstrated and reinforced a few times in the beginning, but resist the urge to continually do it for them. Encourage them to take strong initiative and reach out to their teacher to ask for help. Encourage them to set up regular meeting times with that teacher. In addition, encourage them to discuss and explore different learning approaches they can try to better grasp the material they might be struggling with. The best gifts in life can't be given, they're earned. As a teacher, I can ensure you that nothing is more satisfying to your child (and subsequently you) than to see them independently overcome a challenge with skill sets we've all been fostering in them.

What follows here is a chapter-by-chapter review of this book for teachers, student teachers, and parents. It's meant to serve as a review but can also be used as a preview or study guide.

Chapter 1:

Grit can be taught. If you want to give your kid a life skill that will empower them to achieve anything their heart desires, teach them to stick with work when it gets tough. Demonstrate and vocalize that to them and acknowledge your child when you see them do it.

Using the term "smart" in a flippant way can be damaging. When any parent or teacher inadvertently says, "you're so smart," or "that person is so smart," it often deemphasizes the personal insight, fortitude and hard work one had to do to make that achievement. It attributes success to a natural gift that came free of charge. Even if something was easy for a person to achieve, they had to recognize and leverage their own strengths in order to achieve it.

If that term is thrown around without regard to the aforementioned, then your child could start seeing things that way as well, a way in which "they either have it or don't." In other words, they are either smart or they aren't.

However, the earlier one effectively uses the term "smart" around an impressionable young mind, the better. And it's never too late to start. Early on, offer the life nourishing idea that a smart and successful person leveraged their strengths and put in a lot of work and effort to achieve what they did.

193

Remind your child of the personal strengths you see in them on a regular basis. Everyone has personal strengths – EVERYONE. Do they speak (even partially) another language, do they make people laugh, can they mimic other people or animals well, or always seem to remember a line in a movie or what someone said, do they recall the score of the super bowl five years ago, etc.? All these seemingly "insignificant" examples provide glimpses into a world of untapped potential that lies within their own mind. If you draw attention to it, if you call it out. if you help them recognize it, then you are leading them through a small window into that unchartered world.

As a parent, you are one of the strongest influences on them when it comes to how they define "smart." Use your power wisely. Remember that first principal I had whom I quoted in the book (see Ch. 1, p 15)? He's dyslexic and had an extremely tough time reading and succeeding in school, especially in the '80s before special education services were up to par. However, he can relate to and inspire anyone he comes in contact with. THAT'S intelligent. THAT'S smart. As a child, though, his academic success wasn't confirming that truth. His experiences in the Marine Corp, later in life as a teacher, a principal and now as a highly successful superintendent, reinforced the fact that his interpersonal and intra-personal intelligence were off the charts. Imagine if he didn't have those necessary challenging experiences in the

Corp (along with an insightful mother who also worked in education) to help him form that grit and make those self-discoveries about his own natural gifts? Who knows where he'd be.

Avoid, at all costs, speaking negatively about any teacher with your kids, even if the teacher does seem to be at fault. If your child either consciously or subconsciously develops a negative image of their teacher, it will contribute to them closing off their heart and mind to learning what they can from them. It will hurt them in more ways than you could imagine.

If you see your child struggling in a particular teacher's class, try instead complimenting the teacher in a way that combines what your child is specifically struggling with and a valuable opportunity for them to grow, learn and develop their own self attributes. Compliment teachers for providing challenging material, for keeping solid deadlines, or for any strategy they use that might not automatically be resonating or "working" for your child. Your child will automatically understand that the onus is on them to adapt, to recommit, and to persevere through the challenge. Can you think of any life skill that's more valuable?

While working in a highly affluent, private school provides students with a lot of advantages, the largest disadvantage I've seen is when parents get overly involved and attempt to negotiate grades, deadlines, school rules, etc. on their child's behalf.

While these particular types of parents believe they are acting in their kids' best interest, the result is the exact opposite. It consciously and subconsciously strips their own kids from the important challenges and life lessons that are needed to develop perseverance, grit and onus to see a problem through. Taking away these kinds of challenging experiences from your child, which are necessary experiences to discover themselves, are damaging to their own growth and maturity.

Remind your kids that the people (faculty, principals, staff, etc.) in the school, not the school itself, is what ultimately contributes to their growth and getting the most out of their education (See Ch1). Remind them that struggle is necessary and that if they're not struggling, then they're not growing and learning. In every teacher's career, we see a few students a year who have the misconception that they would be doing better if they were in another school. While that might be true in certain cases where highly specialized services are needed, it's rarely true for any other reason. Keeping your child's focus on the people who are working in the school, instead of the school itself, will humanize that school system and make it more approachable for them.

PARENT TAKEAWAYS
- Use the term "smart" in a context which emphasizes self-understanding and grit.
- Acknowledge and reward your child's personal effort over an accomplishment.

- Only use positive reinforcement to change behavior; do not use punishment.

STUDENT TAKEAWAYS
• Recognizing the goodness in your teachers will make you more receptive to learning.
• Your heart is connected to your mind.
• Make the distinction between your teachers and the physical school where they work.
• Teachers and schools aren't automatically provided to all kids in the world.

Chapter 2: The Value of Mindset

Help your child develop a "growth" mindset by complimenting effort, not outcome. As Zen Tao philosophy supports, help them to take pleasure in their own journey, not the destination. When your child does well on an exam, paper, or speech, resist the urge to say "you're so smart," and instead compliment either the effort or personal strength (hopefully both) they utilized to achieve that outcome. Compliment resiliency, courage and hard work in others as well. Do it often. When your child sees other people's achievements as a result of the effort they made versus the natural born talent they have, then they will have acquired a concrete tool to make those same connections to achievement for themselves.

You don't need something tangible, like an A paper to compliment, to help your child adapt this mindset. The challenge doesn't have to be boring and unpleasant for them either. If your child is enjoying something (e.g., playing a video game for hours even though they can't get passed one particular level), they're going to keep doing it, even if it's difficult. Helping them to make a connection between a task and the innate faculties they possess to accomplish that task will help lead them to more enjoyment, and as a result, more fortitude toward any challenge they're working through.

Draw attention to typical, every day events that make them unique–such as the fact that they always seem to recall Grandma's stories in such vivid detail, or that they can figure out any electronic gadget, or that they remember melodies of songs so well, etc. Take it a step further and try to define the innate strength they have (interpersonal, kinesthetic, musical intelligence, etc.) that allowed them to do it. Remind them (often) that they can capitalize on that natural strength to learn other things, to learn ANYTHING. Offer ideas on how they might apply that strength toward a challenging task. Encourage them to talk to their teachers about trying that method. By doing this, you're showing them a process to self-analyze and take advantage of how their own particular brain processes and learns information. The more they do it, the more fortitude and enjoyment they will have with learning challenges.

Get your child thinking about how their own mind works. Encourage them to self-analyze by looking at past and present events that provide glimpses into specific strengths. It's a fun conversation to have! Talk about how your own mind works, as opposed to their dad, as opposed to their grandmother, or sibling or friend. Tell a story about your own parent, something you'd never forget, which points out how their brain was uniquely different. Point out these differences in the same way you'd differentiate physical appearances between two people. By doing this, you're consciously and subconsciously reminding them that everyone's brain works differently. You're reminding them that even when a task seems impossible, their own unique mind has its own unique way to find a successful outcome, even though their approach may be very different than someone else.

PARENT TAKEAWAYS
- Recognize and acknowledge the individual strengths not only in your child's mind, but in others as well.
- Suggest practical, action driven ways for your child to leverage their personal learning strengths.
- Compliment effort over outcome.

STUDENT TAKEAWAYS
- Adopt a growth mindset in which you know your time and effort are worthwhile.
- Leverage your personal strengths by utilizing learning techniques that complement them.
- Develop the courage to self-analyze regularly.

Chapter 3: Intrapersonal Fuels all Intelligences

Teachers love to see students learn. Therefore, any teacher would welcome a unique tip or idea not only on how a particular students mind processes information to help them learn, but how to motivate them. While that teacher might not be able to incorporate that specific technique into their specific lesson plan for the day, they most definitely will be able to offer ideas on how to incorporate that idea into the larger picture and end goal. In addition, if the teacher is able to tap into some of those personal motivations early on, then they can use massive leverage to help your child succeed.

Remember that opportunities to succeed are extremely motivating. Don't be surprised to see your child gain considerable momentum in terms of their own effort, focus and grit as they discover and share the inner faculties of their own mind. Success comes in many forms though, so don't just wait for the big accomplishments to compliment.

Recognizing and celebrating smaller successes (whether a small hurdle was overcome or your child demonstrates the grit to continue trying to overcome it) will have the same positive effect. So start now. That approach will put your child on a path of self-analysis quicker and you will soon discover that the inner drive in them starts taking over … and that you can't turn it off even if you try. So, encourage your child to make an appointment with their teacher, especially to discuss how their own mind processes best. The teacher will, in turn, be able to match pedagogical tools and make suggestions that compliments their own particular strengths.

My interpretation of the definition of insanity (doing the same thing that doesn't work over and over again) is analogous with a life unanalyzed. If any student of life continually takes the same approach to a problem or challenge without using informative feedback on how to modify their approach, without any success and without any enjoyment, then they are unaware of how to fully engage and leverage their own natural gifts. If they're not aware or being encouraged to leverage what they do have, then they can completely disengage with the learning process as a life norm. Unfortunately, I've seen this happen too many times, with both students and adult friends who have extremely talented minds but have disengaged with the joy of learning to such an extent that it's haltered the success, enjoyment and fulfillment they deserve out of life. Leveraging personal strengths with a creative approach takes some self-analysis and time, but it is time well spent. Once they get in the habit of it, their whole attitude toward life can change because it can bring them closer to their own sense of purpose.

PARENT TAKEAWAYS
- Encourage your child (especially teenagers) to avoid the "insanity" definition by continuing to

try new approaches to challenging tasks with an emphasis on leveraging their personal strengths.
- Help your child develop a time and place to self-reflect; it rarely comes naturally.
- Point out the positive, direct applications that resulted from any self-discoveries they made about their own mind toward tangible learning challenges.
- Encourage any and all of your child's new ideas and approaches toward learning challenges, even if they seem strange or different.

STUDENT TAKEAWAYS
- Recognize the multitude of ways in which you can be "smart."
- Identify your strongest personal "intelligences."
- Explore specific learning processes to unlock your potential.
- Find endless motivation within yourself by knowing yourself.

Chapter 4: Bloom's Taxonomy

Remind your child that the only way to truly learn something is by doing it, even if the "doing" part is engaging in a new learning process. At the top of Bloom's Taxonomy, a basic hierarchical pyramid illustrating educational objectives (see Ch. 4, p. 43), you'll see words like create, analyze, apply and evaluate. At the bottom you'll see memorization. How fun was it for you to memorize and then try to factually recall information? We've all had to do it at times, but the truth is we probably can't even tell you those times because those facts are long forgotten!

When you engage in a discussion with your child about making sense of new information and applying it in a meaningful way, then you're subconsciously prompting them to move up Bloom's taxonomy to exercise their own higher order thinking skills. You're also prompting them to have more fun with the learning process. They'll be processing on a high level in that very moment.

Keeping your focus and praise on your child's attempts to make sense of and apply new information in a meaningful way will also prompt them to explore what personally works for them, which, once again, leads them down a road of self-discovery and opens the door to using new learning techniques. As they find what works for them, they will naturally stick with a task longer and develop a sense of perseverance, especially when it gets challenging. Just think—if they are encouraged to approach all new learning obligations in that way, then they will (eventually) master whatever particular skillset is needed for that task. Do it often enough, and the only possible outcome is an increase in confidence and grit. That alone is a more valuable life trait than anything else they can pick up from their schooling.

Remember, while it is tempting to simply compliment good grades alone (and yes, a good grade on any given assignment CAN reflect mastery of a particular skillset), the focus should be on the skills they acquired and the effective work method they put in to achieve that grade. So, if you're going to compliment an A on an English paper, make sure you keep the focus on the particular writing techniques they leveraged, the hard work they put in, and the subsequent skills they acquired to get that A, not the grade itself. That approach will emphasize the broader picture which is the real point of schooling–to prepare your child for life.

Encourage your child to talk about what they are learning in school. Show interest, even if what they're discussing sounds foreign or boring (or both) to you. You don't have to be an expert in that subject to help them form valuable connections that can empower them to learn more effectively. Try using the "this reminds me of" approach. If your child is discussing a problem in calculus and you've always hated Math, it will still remind you of something. Point out that something, whether it was particular problems in Math you personally struggled with, a student you remember who was a Math wizard, or the teaching approach your instructor took back when you were in school. That discussion alone consciously and subconsciously reminds your child that all minds work differently and emphasizes the importance of being aware and awake to the various instructional methods available to them to master any given task. In addition, it's synthesizing and analyzing that information in a different way. Everyone can get to the finish line in a different way. Your child needs to understand that.

PARENT TAKEAWAYS
- Show your child that learning can be fun by prompting them to apply and evaluate information, not just memorize.
- Have confidence that your child's creative forces, both in terms of their own new learning techniques and their own new ideas based on acquired knowledge, will come more naturally if they're consistently encouraged to explore and apply their natural abilities.

STUDENT TAKEAWAYS
- Apply and analyze all new information you receive to understand it better.
- Connect new ideas to things you already know.
- Have more fun while learning by taking initiative to exercise your higher order thinking skills.

Chapter 5 Kinesthetic Intelligence

If your child can't sit still and they love to hike, bike, swim, play sports, dance, fidget with objects, etc., then they are probably in that popular category of kinesthetic learner. Encourage them to create their own hands-on experiences whenever possible. They can role play when learning about people in history or reading Shakespeare in English. See if they can borrow a molecular model kit from their teacher or buy a used one (very cheap on Amazon) in Chemistry. Get them to try manipulating objects (toothpicks, beans, etc.) in Math, or simply encourage them to get on their feet when trying to internalize new information rather than passively studying notes and/or reading text while sitting.

It's been confirmed countless times during my teaching career that this type of learner will always do better on their feet, even if some sort of manipulative object isn't available. Therefore, accompanying some auditory feedback (listening to taped notes, having a discussion, speaking the steps through a mathematical calculation, etc.) works very well and is much more effective and time efficient than simple sitting and reading. If that inevitable (but hopefully rare) time to cram for an assessment does come, this technique alone can be a time efficient life saver for them.

I've had a few insightful students in the past ask me if it's okay if they periodically stand in back of the class during specific times when they're required to sit to take notes or an exam. Ironically, those same students were previously labeled as "trouble makers." However, making those easy seating modifications turned out to be well worth it.

Those same students not only didn't abuse the privilege they were given, but they were vastly more productive, efficient and engaged during class. Remind your child that it's always possible to modify certain classroom protocols and structure if they talk with their instructor and demonstrate a sincere desire and rationale to do so. It not only will help your child stay focused, but it will increase their own self-knowledge (intrapersonal intelligence) and give them a process for negotiating learning situations that aren't immediately in their favor.

Above all, encourage them to have fun while they're doing it. Want to see your child procrastinate less and take more onus for their responsibilities? Then show them that performing the tasks they're responsible for, even if it's in a subject they despise, doesn't have to be a dreadful experience.

For most learners, even if you're not high in kinesthetic aptitude, getting your hands on something to learn is fun. Helping them to find that joy in learning (and yes, it can still be turned around in high school even if your child has formed a negative association with school and/or learning) also starts pushing them into a "growth" mindset. Thus, they will see efforts they make as worthwhile. Remind and encourage them to get moving… literally.

PARENT TAKEAWAYS
- Encourage your child to speak to their instructor about making some easy class modifications to suit their kinesthetic aptitude
- If they're working at home, encourage your child

to stand, walk, stretch and move as they study.
- Suggest common household items to empower a tactile experience if they're struggling with understanding concepts.

STUDENT TAKEAWAYS
- Use various forms of movement to stimulate learning and activate memory.
- Explore with your hands to gain more information.
- Playing and having fun also equates to powerful learning.

Chapter 6: Interpersonal Intelligence

Here's when having that talk with your child about what they're learning in school pays off in more ways than one. You already know if your child is high on the interpersonal scale. When was the last time they were able to talk their way out of trouble? Do they have a knack for making people laugh? Do they read people well, adapt to different social situations easily, and are good conversationalists? If you've already thought of several examples which indicates they have a high aptitude for interpersonal intelligence, then remind your child that they have a tremendous strength which can be powerfully utilized to learn difficult information.

Your child will learn more easily if they're able to converse with others about it–even if it's some sort of visual chat with a friend online. It is always better to do it in person though, so if you have that option, encourage it. Having a quiet space to sit down with a study partner is crucial for this kind of learner, so trying to provide that space for them will help tremendously. That being said, students share all sorts of free time (mornings, lunch, free blocks, possibly after school, etc.) while they're at school and should meet with their peers and teachers to study during those times. Getting your child to recognize the value of it might take some consistent encouragement in the beginning, but your effort is worthwhile.

Teachers will always love students who take initiative with their own learning. Scheduling regular sessions to meet with their teacher one-on-one will be of tremendous value for this type of learner. If your child develops the habit of meeting with their teacher regularly (5-10-minute weekly check in is all that's needed), not only will it have a tremendous advantage in terms of content comprehension, but the bond between them and their teacher will grow stronger.

If your child is fairly new to the idea of regularly using study partners to comprehend content, then it will take some initial effort, along with some trial and error (not all study partners will work out). Their main choice of a study partner should never be based on who their closest friend is, but on whom they think they can learn from the most. Picking a best friend to study with can sometimes be extremely unproductive in terms of grasping class content. Even though your child is aware of that, I've found consistent reminders are often needed for them to truly internalize that fact.

It also helps to be in the habit of starting each singular group study session with specific goals and to determine at the end of each session if those goals were met. If they weren't, taking some time to analyze why will help raise your child's awareness on how to structure more effective peer study sessions in the future. Keeping a time log during those peer and/or small group sessions is critical also. That one habit alone will draw needed attention to the value of time and the potential ways in which it can be wasted. Those small habits are very easy to maintain, yet extremely transparent and measurable. If goal and time logging become a habit, efficiency will not only improve within their own group sessions, but they'll more easily recognize when certain teaching methods aren't working for them and how they might employ modifications.

PARENT TAKEAWAYS
- Encourage your child's group study sessions and help them find a place and time for it.
- Facilitate conversations with your child about what they're learning.

- If they're not in the habit of regular study groups, encourage them to take the initial step to schedule it.
- Encourage teacher check-ins.
- Remind your child that their unique brain will have more fun and be more efficient if they embrace study groups.

STUDENT TAKEAWAYS
- Create structured study time with friends, peers and colleagues to learn more easily.
- Initiate content specific conversations with others to process information.
- Role play, create simulations, and Facetime chat when you can't meet in person.

Chapter 7: Visual – Spatial Intelligence

All students benefit from visual instruction, but there are certain students who can't grasp a concept without it. If your child struggles a lot with understanding content from text, but instead needs to "see it," then encourage them to create an environment that feeds that powerful gateway. That environment goes well beyond wherever they sleep at night. It starts with the way their desktop is set up on their laptop, or how digital folders, binders and their own bag is organized. It even includes how they organize learning videos on YouTube or other search engines on any given computer. While technology will always offer great additional options for visual spatial learners, the way this type of learner absorbs information will never change. They need visual prompting to process, connect and retain.

Encourage a color-coded environment, whether it's colored "tags" on digital folders, flash cards, or actual folders. Make colored pencils and highlighters easily accessible and put them in your child's bag or binder. Fill notes with sketches and pictures that connect concepts and ideas. For less than $20 on Amazon, you can get a good whiteboard that you can keep at home. Some whiteboards are small and designed to carry in a bag and take up much less room than a textbook.

One quick glance at your child's "environment" (their room, bag, desktop, etc.) will quickly clue you in on if they're leveraging this particular strength to the fullest capacity. These visual tools are just as necessary to your child as the right sized Philips head screwdriver is for a matching screw and should be sought after by your child regularly. If a student has trouble getting these tools on their own, any teacher would be happy to help them find a way.

Your child's workspace at home is just as important. They do not need a large space, but they do need to have a space to work and be creative with these tools and visual cues. It doesn't have to be fancy in the least, it just has to tap into their visual-spatial senses.

In addition, asking your child to "describe what they see" is a great prompt for them to retrieve and process information from memory, assuming they had previously worked with some sort of visual cue to begin with. When you see your child making efforts to create that space in any way, then you're witnessing an evolving mind and it's time for a celebratory acknowledgment.

Technology plays right into the hands of a visual spatial learner if they use it wisely. Most students are carrying some sort of smart phone, the equivalent of a mini computer, in their pocket. Taking pictures of ideas on a board or watching a video of steps involved in equation solving could be extremely useful. It shouldn't replace the real-time processing these students need to go through when taking notes (drawing images, highlighting, etc.), but it's an excellent supplement. Also, search engines make it easy for anyone. Type almost any content-driven idea into a search engine, click on images and you'll see some sort of concept map that relates to it.

Making a technology supplement a habit could alone increase retention and decrease processing time by half. Obviously, this practice exposes them to a whole new set of problems in terms of distraction spanning from social media to excessive texting and any and all between. Studies even support that too much of it compromises the quality of sleep and contributes to social isolation. Therefore, educating and bringing awareness to the pitfalls of overindulging in these distractions is mandatory.

Having worked with thousands of students coming from both extreme ends of the financial spectrum, I know that the extent to which a home space or technology supplement can be provided will vary. Even if a small visual learning space at home isn't possible, a public and/or school library with the aforementioned visual tools in their bag will provide all the necessary learning tricks for their minds to flourish. Remember, small tools and habits lead to big results.

PARENT TAKEAWAYS
- Recognize and support the value of visual tools for your child.
- Encourage students to utilize technology, already in their possession, in a responsible way.
- Prompt them with "describe what you see."

STUDENT TAKEAWAYS
- Map out concepts and big ideas and draw pictures to represent information.
- Use symbols while taking notes and a highlighter when reading text.
- Color code information with different colored pencils, highlighters or notecards, especially when preparing for assessments.
- Watch teaching videos.

Chapter 8 Linguistic Intelligence

Accessibility to recording devices has never been more prevalent for your kids. It's available on all cell phones, laptops, digital devices, etc. If you and your child have recognized a high aptitude for linguistic learning, then recording lectures and/or reading their own class notes, ideas, questions, etc. into a recorder is a necessary part of their process. The second important piece of that process is listening back. For them, it's much more powerful than reading that same information. So, having and using a good pair of headphones is an essential tool. I suggest having two pair, one in their pocket and another pair in their bag. Having that pair of headphones should be as common as a pair of keys, wallet or phone. It's never forgotten.

In addition, simply initiating a discussion about what your child is learning in class will feed this faculty. When students with high levels of linguistic intelligence speak and hear ideas and concepts, especially challenging ones, then they are processing in that moment. Encourage conversations about undesirable subjects as much as their favorite ones. While it might take some prodding to get to that one subject or class they least enjoy, it will be worth it. Your child does not need answers spelled out for them, they need linguistic processing to continually move toward better understanding. Conversing out loud gives them a way to move toward better understanding and self-discover their own sources of confusion while forming the right questions. It's a necessary process that only gets more efficient with consistent effort.

Want to get your child smiling about what they're doing in terms of their own efficient learning? Ask them to share a memory mnemonic (See Ch 8, p. 86), rhyme or song they're using to remember information that's hard to recall. If they don't have one, ask them what they're waiting for! Offer a silly idea or come up with a mnemonic together for some content-driven information they're responsible for knowing. That single act can help relieve stress for a child who is struggling and remind them that learning doesn't have to be painful. Remember, habits of work and mind and a consistent effort, in the right manner, is what will open your child up to their unlimited (yet specific) potential and personal joy.

PARENT TAKEAWAYS
- Initiate conversations with you child about what they're learning, both in and out of school.
- Use mnemonics in your own home to model and demonstrate effectiveness.
- Encourage them to create listening opportunities out of reading assignments.

STUDENT TAKEAWAYS
- Record class lectures and read information into a recording device on a regular basis.
- Use headphones to listen to information throughout your busy day.
-

- Use mnemonic devices, verbal debates, songs and rhymes to process and remember.

Chapter 9: Habits of Work and Mind

Habits of work and mind are heavily influenced by the people your child is surrounded by. While we lose more and more time with our own kids the older they get, we can still have a positive influence by connecting with the people they spend time with the most. Taking that moment to introduce yourself to your child's teachers, coaches, mentors and friends is worth it. I'm by no means encouraging overinvolvement, or taking care of tasks that your child should be doing on their own. I'm emphasizing the importance of being close to those people in your child's life so you can understand where influences are coming from and reach out to them if needed.

"If needed" is probably one of the more subjective phrases a parent can hear and it's interpretation will differ depending on which parent you're speaking to. In my experience, if you see a distinct negative change in behavior or a bad pattern that's become habitual, or if your child is truly struggling with motivation, then it's time to reach out to those people. Of course, that's in addition to the scheduled check-ins all schools have, such as parent-teacher night, report cards, discussions and comments that teachers have initiated, etc. Ultimately, it's that team of people who surround your child throughout their day which will contribute to their habits of work and mind.

Allow your child to make mistakes—often. It is the only true way they will develop the resiliency which builds strong and effective habits of work and mind. Resist the urge to do something that your child can do for themselves, especially by the time they get into high school. If you are reaching out to teachers to request extensions for your child, to find out the latest scores on assessments, to negotiate grades, etc., then you are robbing your child of the necessary experiences they need to truly take on the onus of their own educational (not just academic) life and to flourish. It's not easy to do when you want to "help," and it takes a lot of restraint, so try to remember the reasons behind what your child may interpret as your inaction to a problem they're experiencing. Instead, remind them of the importance of learning to independently cope with that situation and suggest some steps they can and should take on their own.

Encourage your child to discuss and think through bigger decisions and/or problems. Clarity is often partially achieved simply by articulating what the problem is. Further, if they can hear you or another mentor's ideas on the matter, it will then model a way for them to engage in deeper level thinking themselves. You'd be surprised how much "real time" processing happens in those types of moments by teenagers.

PARENT TAKEAWAYS
- Stay connected to the people who spend the most time with your child.
- Allow your child to make mistakes. Ultimately, it's how they will learn and grow the most.
- Encourage self-reliance.

STUDENT TAKEAWAYS
- Hope and grit can be borrowed, learned and taught.
- Avoid negative thought patterns and negative people.
- Take initiative toward being self-reliant and don't be afraid to make mistakes.
- Ask yourself if there is more to consider when making decisions.
- Develop perseverance by sticking with challenging and boring tasks.
- Incorporate an organizational system that's easy to maintain and commit to it.
- Monitor when your concentration deviates in order to improve it.
- How you express yourself is governed by the environment you're in.

Chapter 10: Assessment

In my 15-year teaching career, I have never seen more anxiety among students than in these past few years. Now more than ever, coping mechanisms are necessary and one of the best ways to cope with any situation that causes anxiety is through preparation. So, if your child experiences test anxiety, encourage them to set up mock situations for themselves. Speak as if it's a necessary (not optional) process to prepare for any approaching written test. How they set up a practice test is up to them, but labeling that specific task as a requirement helps draw their attention to the importance of it.

If your child can build that one technique into their preparation routine, it not only will help them perform better on the specific test they're preparing for, but it will help them become a better test taker in general. After all, part of that process requires them to come up with possible test questions which fosters their ability to identify important information. The residual effect of this technique is decreased anxiety because they're more familiar with what to expect on the day.

When it comes to consistent success on any written assessment, organization is vital. It takes boys longer to develop the important executive functioning skills needed to keep track of educational responsibilities, so keep a closer eye on them when it comes to organization. A quick glance at whatever organizational system they've established is all that's needed.

While many options are available for them to do this, a smart phone (if they have one) will probably make the most sense. How do they keep track of assignment, assessment and homework dates? More importantly, how do they consistently check in on what they're learning in each course?

Some sort of daily content reminder for each class, even if they have nothing tangible to hand in, helps keep the information relevant and approachable in their mind. It's especially helpful if your child is on some sort of rotating block schedule and does not have the same class every day.

In addition, what does their bag and binder look like? Organization is a skill they have to learn, so a quick glance with a possible organizational suggestion is all that's needed on your part. Your check-in is just a reinforcement of the team's (who are the people surrounding your child throughout the course of their day) initiative to help them develop good habits of work and mind.

Encourage your child to speak to their teachers before and after tests and quizzes. Remind them that teachers love when students show initiative. Very often, teachers will provide students with more specific tips on how to prepare for an exam if a student goes out of their way to ask. It also will greatly reduce a student's anxiety level to get more familiar with what to expect. Understanding where they made mistakes on passed exams is just as important. Hopefully, your child's teacher will have reviewed all sources of confusion on passed written assessments for the class as a whole, but if they don't, or if your child happened to be absent that particular day, it's imperative that they follow up. It not only helps clarify misconceptions on that particular question, but provides valuable clues to that instructor's line of questioning for future assessments.

Take occasional notice of the method your child is using to prepare for a quiz or test. Ask them why they chose that particular way. Just by asking the question, it draws attention to the importance of method as much as content. Not all preparation methods are best for your child, so stay open minded to their exploration of technique and their chosen approach. At the same time, don't be afraid to call them out if you notice a very obvious distraction compromising their concentration. While these suggestions might seem like I'm encouraging micromanagement, it's actually the opposite. They should be done occasionally (few times a month) and quickly. The goal is to reinforce the development of their own skillset at mastering true educational independence.

PARENT TAKEAWAYS
- Encourage your child to speak to their teachers before and after written assessments.
- Instill that it's expected for them to clarify all misconceptions on big assessments.
- Support your child's attempts to create mock testing situations.

STUDENT TAKEAWAYS
- Practice strong, consistent habits of work and mind to learn better and avoid heavy cram sessions.
- Tests (especially standardized) are often a skill in

test taking itself, regardless of content.
- Eliminate distractions and choose the right environment when studying.
- If forced to cram, use the 50-10 rule, along with rewriting and clustering techniques.
- Grades can be negotiated.

Chapter 11: Anxiety:

We've already discussed the importance of taking a look at your child's preparation methods to minimize their own anxiety, but there are some additional ways you can help. If your child is expressing concern or complaining about any academic challenge they're having, then it's causing them stress. Listen to the problem and if you're making suggestions always make sure they're in the form of action-driven steps that are within your child's control. Focusing too much of the conversation on what is not within their control could actually foster even more anxiety and enable behavior that isn't serving them.

You know your child best. Some need very little pushing and seem to be self-motivated, and some might take more work, a lot more work. Regardless of where they fall on this spectrum, encouraging them to be deliberate about incorporating a regular and effective means of stress management is important. Just like various learning techniques, if the idea of self-care is new to them, it might take some exploration on their part to find what works.

While I will always be a fan of students detaching from technology completely and engaging in exercise, yoga, meditation or a walk outside, some new studies are starting to reveal that video games can actually put people in a good mood and have positive psychological benefits. I take those studies with a grain of salt because of the sheer time consumption video games can take.

My personal experience is hard core "gamers" are often not putting enough time and effort into the academic work across all content areas because they have a lack of time and brain space to do so. Therefore, my suggestion is to ask your child an honest question—do you think playing video helps you maintain stress levels? Get them thinking about it. Have clear time limits and restrictions if your child does like to play video games and stick to it.

PARENT TAKEAWAYS

- Refocus your child's attention on action driven steps that are within their control to reduce anxiety.
- Encourage deliberate, conscious, consistent engagement in forms of relaxation that personally resonate with your child.
- Talk it out with them when they're feeling stressed.
- Set up restrictions on "relaxation time" if it's being abused.

STUDENT TAKEAWAYS

- Thorough preparation helps to greatly reduce anxiety.
- Do not worry or waste energy on that which is not within your control.
- Employ a regular meditative practice into your life.

Chapter 12: Life Applications, not just grades

To state the obvious, recognizing, acknowledging and encouraging your child's natural strengths are vitally important, in addition to being fun. As they discover and leverage these strengths, it enables them, on so many levels, to see how they could be of use to others and to the world. It's this purpose that feeds their own motivation and empowers them to increase a sense of self-worth. Encourage your child to find purpose in everything they do, especially when facing challenges in school or elsewhere. Pointing out the bigger picture (i.e. connecting their ability to overcome educational challenges to overcoming life challenges) will help them see the purpose in what they're presently doing in terms of their own work, whether it be in school or elsewhere. Most importantly, encourage them to give of themselves to help others. It's the truest way they'll discover their own potential.

PARENT TAKEAWAYS

- Demonstrate philanthropy and generosity of spirit

to empower your own child.
- Connect your child's strengths to potential ways it can serve others and the world.

STUDENT TAKEAWAYS
- Education is vital to overcome pain and suffering.
- You experience more joy in life, have more love to give, and form more meaningful relationships when you live your life with purpose.
- Use your own innate faculties to help others.
- The power of prayer is scientifically proven.
- Wear your seatbelt.